WHAT DOES THE BIBLE REALLY SAY?

ADDRESSING REVISIONIST ARGUMENTS ON SEXUALITY AND THE BIBLE

MARTIN DAVIE

The Latimer Trust

ISBN 978-1-906327-67-5

Cover photo: Adam and Eve and the Original Sin by jorisvo on AdobeStock.

Published by the Latimer Trust December 2020. This publication has been assisted by a donation from CEEC.

The Latimer Trust (formerly Latimer House, Oxford) is a conservative Evangelical research organisation within the Church of England, whose main aim is to promote the history and theology of Anglicanism as understood by those in the Reformed tradition. Interested readers are welcome to consult its website for further details of its many activities.

The Latimer Trust

London N14 4PS UK

Registered Charity: 1084337

Company Number: 4104465

Web: www.latimertrust.org

E-mail: administrator@latimertrust.org

CONTENTS

Introduction

One of the responsibilities given to Christians is to 'contend for the faith that was once for all delivered to the saints' (Jude 3). There is a pattern of authoritative teaching that was given by Christ to the apostles and which they then handed on the church and Christians are called by God to contend on behalf of this pattern of teaching when it comes under attack.[1]

This pattern of teaching has been attacked in many different ways during the history of the church, but in our day one of the key areas in which it has come under attack is the area of human sexuality. The historic Christian position on human sexuality, which has been upheld by Roman Catholics, the Orthodox, Protestants and Pentecostals alike is now under attack not only from those outside the church, but also from those inside the church who are seeking to revise its teaching to conform to the mores of contemporary Western society.[2]

In 2019, as part of the attack on the historic Christian position from inside the Church of England, the website ViaMedia.News posted a series of ten articles under the general heading, 'Does the Bible Really Say...?' These articles were posted between 17 May and 18 July 2019 and they were written by seven writers: Dr Jonathan Tallon, Dr Meg Warner, Professor Martyn Percy, Bishop David Gillett, Mr Marcus Greene, Dr Hayley Matthews and Dr Simon Taylor. This book is a collection of the responses to these articles which were originally posted on my blog, *Reflections of an Anglican*

---

[1] For this point, see Martin Davie, 'How do we know what the faith is?' in Paul Fiddes (ed.), *Sharing the Faith at the Boundaries of Unity* (Oxford: Regents Park College, 2015), pp. 8–15.

[2] C S Lewis gives a helpful summary of this historic position in chapters 5 and 6 of his book, *Mere Christianity* (Glasgow: Fontana, 1984).

Theologian, and then on the website of the Church of England Evangelical Council.[1]

As we shall see in more detail in the subsequent chapters of this book, the ViaMedia.News articles put forward ten basic arguments:

1. While the New Testament condemns pederasty (i.e. sexual intercourse between men and boys) it says nothing about the sort of loving consensual homosexual relationships we know today.

2. The foundation for the biblical rejection of extra-marital sex is Deuteronomy 22:13–29, a text which reflects a view of women as the property of men which we no longer accept today.

3. The Bible gives us not one but several different patterns of marriage.

4. God created some people to be gay or lesbian and God regards same-sex sexual relationships as wholesome.

5. The story of Sodom is not about same-sex relationships. It is about rape, or people using sex to try to become divine, or a story in which Lot misunderstands a request from the Sodomites to know who his visitors are.

6. Romans 1:18–32 only refers to the sexual activity of 'broken' gay people and 1 Corinthians 6:9–11 is about the immoral actions of straight mem. Paul's big vision is of a new community in which everyone is welcome, and we should not say that gay people need to be sexually abstinent to be part of it.

7. Families can take many forms and a family does not need to have a 'mummy and daddy'.

---

[1] See *Reflections of An Anglican Theologian* at https://mbarrattdavie.wordpress.com/; and CEEC website at http://www.ceec.info (accessed 13 April 2020).

8. The church is a society created by adoption, for which the existence of traditional 'nuclear' families should no longer be important.

9. The Church of England takes an inclusive approach to the 'foundation sacrament' of baptism in that it welcomes everyone, including gay people and their children. It is therefore ironic that it bars gay people from marriage or the possibility of ordination.

10. The Bible does not support a 'complementarian understanding of creation' in which humans are 'made and meant to be male and female'.

As we shall also see in the chapters that follow, all these arguments for a revision of the historic Christian position on human sexuality are seriously mistaken.

- The New Testament says nothing specifically about pederasty, but what it does do is reject all forms of same-sex sexual activity (including *inter alia* loving, consensual same-sex relationships) on the basis that God has ordained marriage between one man and one woman as the context for human sexual activity to take place.

- Neither Deuteronomy 22:13–29, nor any other biblical text, sees women as the property of men and the foundation for the prohibition of extra-marital sexual activity is not Deuteronomy 22, but the way humanity has been created by God as witnessed to in the creation accounts in Genesis 1 and 2, in Jesus' teaching in Matthew 19:3-9 and Mark 10:2-9, and in Paul's teaching in Ephesians 5:31-32.

- It is not true that there are several different patterns of marriage in the Bible. There are two (both heterosexual in nature) – monogamy and polygyny. The former is the normative pattern instituted by God at creation; the latter is rare and is both explicitly prohibited in Old Testament law and implicitly condemned by the way it is depicted in the biblical narratives.

- Both our natural knowledge of human biology and the teaching of Scripture contradict the idea that some people are created by God to be lesbian or gay and Scripture provides no support for the idea that God regards same-sex sexual relationships as 'wholesome'.

- The story of Sodom in Genesis 19 is not about rape, nor about people wanting to become divine, nor about an unfortunate misunderstanding between Lot and the other inhabitants of Sodom. It is about the men of Sodom wanting to have homosexual sex with Lot's two visitors. It is this desire for homosexual sexual activity that confirms the great wickedness of Sodom and the neighbouring cities and leads to their destruction by the judgement of God.

- Romans 1:18–32 is not concerned with the sexual activities of a special subset of broken gay people. It depicts lesbian and gay sexual activity as such as a clear manifestation of the fact that the human race as a whole has turned away from God. In addition, scholarly study of the terms *malakoi* and *arsenokoitai* used in 1 Corinthians 6:9 has established that they refer to the passive and active partners in male same-sex unions. Paul does indeed have a vision of a new community open to all, but his letters show that he expects the members of that community to adhere to an ethic of sexual faithfulness within (heterosexual) marriage and sexual abstinence outside it.

- While families do take a range of different forms, the Bible tells us that the form of family life ordained by God is that in which there is a father and a mother who are married to each other. What is more, decades of research have consistently shown that this form of family life is that one that is most conducive to human well-being.

- The fact that the church is a family formed by people being adopted into a relationship with God through Christ does not negate the continuing importance of 'nuclear' families consisting of fathers and mothers and their children. God has created both the supernatural family of the church and natural human families and Christians are called to respect the vital importance of both.

- The Church of England's current approach to baptising those in same-sex relationships and their children is based on the flawed teaching of *Issues in Human Sexuality* that same-sex relationships are acceptable for lay people providing they conscientiously believe that this is what is right for them.[2] There needs to be a properly informed discussion about the matter which focuses on the question of whether being in a lesbian or gay relationship necessarily precludes the repentance that is required of those who bring children to baptism or who seek baptism for themselves.

- The Bible does support a 'complementarian' view of creation in the sense that from Genesis 1 and 2 onwards it consistently holds that God has created human beings as male and female and that to live rightly means to live in the light of this truth. There are a tiny number of intersex people who combine male and female characteristics in their biology and so are both male and female. However, even the disorder of their sexual development points to the truth that human beings have been created by God to be a sexually dimorphic species.

The title of the ViaMedia.News series, 'Does the Bible Really Say....?,' echoes some key words from the narrative of the Fall in Genesis 3. In that narrative, Adam and Eve have been given absolutely clear instructions that they may not eat the fruit of the tree of the knowledge of good and evil for this will bring death. However, Satan, in the form of a snake, asks Eve the question, 'Did God really say, "You must not eat from any tree in the garden?"' (Genesis 3:1). This question sows a seed of doubt that eventually results in the Fall when Eve, and then

---

[2] The Church of England, *Issues in Human Sexuality* (London: Church House Publishing, 1993), pp.41-42.

4

Adam, succumb to the temptation to eat the forbidden fruit. The result is then the tragedy of human existence in alienation from God.

The significance of this narrative for the current debate in the church about human sexuality is that behind this debate is once again the question, 'Did God really say?', God has spoken clearly through both nature and Scripture and has told us that he has created us as male and female and has ordained marriage between one man and one woman as the sole legitimate setting for sexual intercourse to take place. We know that this is what God has told us and yet in the face of pressure from our contemporary culture we are tempted to question whether this is what he really meant.

As in the story of the Fall, giving into this temptation will result in being people being alienated from God, both in this world and in the world to come. It is therefore of the utmost importance that this temptation is resisted. The purpose of this book is to encourage such resistance.

I. Why the Bible Does Talk About Homosexuality...and What it Says

In the first article in the ViaMedia.News series 'Does the Bible Really Say....?', Dr Jonathan Tallon considers the question, 'Does the Bible Really Say...Anything at All about Homosexuality as we Understand it Today?'[1]

Dr Tallon's argument

Dr Tallon notes that there are passages in the New Testament that might appear to show that the Bible clearly prohibits homosexual activity. He writes:

> you open your Bible and are reading 1 Corinthians 6:9, and see a reference to 'homosexual offenders' (NIV) or 'homosexual perverts' (GNB). You read Romans 1:27, and note the reference to 'men committing indecent acts with other men'. And it seems that the plain meaning of Scripture is staring you in the face.
>
> Maybe you'd like it to be otherwise. Maybe you don't understand what's so wrong. But it appears to be the plain meaning of Scripture. The Bible appears to say that being homosexual – gay or lesbian – is not OK.

However, Dr Tallon then goes on to argue that this reading of Scripture is mistaken because it is, in fact, misleading to use the modern term 'homosexuality' when talking about what is said in the New Testament. He gives three reasons why this is the case.

---

[1] Jonathan Tallon, 'Does the Bible Really Say...Anything at All about Homosexuality as we Understand it Today?, 17 May 2019, at https://viamedia.news/2019/05/17/does-the-bible-really-say-anything-at-all-about-homosexuality-as-we-understand-it-today/ (accessed 13 April 2020).

First, when we use the term 'homosexual' we mean someone
who has a sexual orientation to a member of their own sex. By
contrast 'the ancient world was generally uninterested in
questions of orientation, but much more concerned with
questions of action.'[1]

Secondly, in the ancient world 'there was no term for
"homosexual". Terms used defined who was the active,
dominant person and who was classed as the passive,
submissive participant.'[2]

Thirdly, if anyone referred to an adult male having sex with
another male (as in Romans 1:27) the assumption would not be
that that male was another adult:

> the natural assumption would be that the males were
> boys. Other assumptions would include that no equal
> relationship was involved, and that the boy would be
> humiliated. But what would not be assumed is that the
> adult only had intercourse with boys; the listener
> would expect the man also to have intercourse with
> women (slaves and prostitutes) and also would
> assume that the man was married (or would be
> married in the future).[3]

What this all means is that our idea of consenting sex between
two adults with an orientation towards a member of their own
sex cannot be read back into the New Testament.

Dr Tallon's overall conclusion is that:

---

[1] Tallon, 'Does the Bible Really Say...Anything at All about
Homosexuality?'.
[2] Tallon, 'Does the Bible Really Say...Anything at All about
Homosexuality?'.
[3] Tallon, 'Does the Bible Really Say...Anything at All about
Homosexuality?'.

In our modern world, 'homosexuality' might conjure up images of loving couples of the same gender in long term relationships. However, the world of the New Testament had no word for 'homosexuality' and precious little visibility of anything like our image today. For the ancient world, male-male sex meant pederasty, it meant abuse, it meant rape, it was something married men did, and it often involved slaves or prostitutes or slave prostitutes. Do condemnations of that mean that we have to condemn loving, faithful relationships now? What is clear, however, is that the Bible doesn't really say anything at all about homosexuality as we understand it today.[4]

The problems with Dr Tallon's argument

Dr Tallon's argument is a re-presentation of an argument previously put forward by Robin Scroggs – that same-sex activity in the first century and homosexuality today are two different phenomena and that therefore we cannot apply the New Testament's rejection of the former to loving, committed homosexual relationships today.[5] The argument goes like this.

- Homosexuality today means loving couples in long-term relationships

- Same-sex relationships in New Testament times meant married men engaging in violently abusive pederasty

- Therefore, when the New Testament condemns the latter it is not talking about homosexuality as we know it today

There are three major problems with this argument.

---

[4] Tallon, 'Does the Bible Really Say...Anything at All about Homosexuality?'.
[5] Robin Scroggs, *The New Testament and Homosexuality: Contextual Background for Contemporary Debate* (Philadelphia: Fortress Press, 1983).

Homosexuality in the ancient world and today

The first problem with this argument is that it misrepresents both the nature of homosexuality today and the nature of same-sex activity in the ancient world.

The reason it misrepresents the nature of homosexuality today is that the definition of a homosexual is someone who is 'sexually attracted to someone of their own sex'.[6] Homosexuality is the same-sex sexual activity engaged in by such a person and (as in the case of heterosexual sexual activity) this can take many different forms. Loving monogamous same-sex relationships are one form, but they are not the only form that exists today. There are also open relationships, serial relationships and casual one-night stands, sexual activity involving pederasty, abusive sexual activity and sexual activity involving prostitution and even sex slavery. There are also married men (and women) who engage in homosexual sexual activity.

The reason it misrepresents the nature same-sex activity in the ancient world is that it fails to acknowledge the evidence we have that a wide range of different forms of same-sex sexual activity were also known about in the ancient world. This is the point that is made by Mark Smith in his important 1996 article 'Ancient Bisexuality and the interpretation of Romans 1:26–27' in which he rebuts the argument of Scroggs.[7]

Smith notes that in addition to relationships between men and boys, there are also examples from the ancient world of relationships between young adult males, between adult males of unequal age, between adult males of roughly equal age, between adult males who alternated in the roles of 'lover' and 'beloved', and between bisexuals and members of both the

---

[6] 'Homosexual', *The New Oxford Dictionary of English* (Oxford: OUP, 1998) p. 879.

[7] Mark Smith, 'Ancient Bisexuality and the interpretation of Romans 1:26–27', *Journal of the American Academy of Religion*, 64, 1996, pp. 223–256.

same and the opposite sex, with many of these relationships being characterised as stable and long lasting and even as lifelong 'marriages'.

In addition, there were also female same-sex relationships, and these were often relationships of mutual consent in which there was no distinction between those playing the active or passive role, no distinction of age between the women involved, and no question of exploitation.[8]

What the evidence cited by Smith indicates is that the forms of same-sex relationships that were known in the ancient world were fundamentally similar to those known today. Male pederasty was not the only thing that was known about and in fact there was 'a decline in the prominence of pederasty in the last three centuries preceding Paul.'[9]

In his book, *Christianity, Social Tolerance and Homosexuality*, the prominent pro-gay church historian John Boswell warns against the 'seductive danger' for the historian:

> posed by the tendency to exaggerate the differences between homosexuality in previous societies and modern ones. One example of this is the common idea that gay relationships in the ancient world differed from their modern counterparts in that they always involved persons of different ages; an older man (the lover) and a young boy (the beloved).[10]

Like Smith, Boswell argues that there is plenty of evidence that same-sex relationships between adult males (such as

---

[8] For lesbianism in the ancient world see Bernadette Brooten, *Love Between Women: Early Christian Responses to Female Homoeroticism* (Chicago: University of Chicago Press 1996).
[9] Smith, 'Ancient Bisexuality'.
[10] John Boswell, *Christianity, Social Tolerance, and Homosexuality* (Chicago: University of Chicago Press, 1980).

Parmenides and Zenon who were sixty-five and forty) were both common and well known in the ancient world.[11]

What this means is that the idea that the New Testament *must* have been referring to pederasty (because this was the only thing people knew about) is unsustainable.

The New Testament references to same-sex sexual activity

Secondly, there is no evidence from the New Testaments itself to support the argument that when the New Testament refers to same-sex sexual activity it is only, or primarily, pederasty that is in view. There are two types of reference to same-sex sexual activity in the New Testament.

The first is the references to *porneia* in texts such as Mark 7:21, Acts 15:20, 1 Corinthians 6:18 and Galatians 5:19. *Porneia* was a comprehensive term which was used to refer to all sexual acts outside of heterosexual marriage.[12] Therefore, in telling Christians to 'shun *porneia*' (1 Corinthians 6:18, NRSVA), the New Testament declares all forms of same-sex sexual activity (and not just pederasty) off limits.

The second is the specific references to same-sex sexual activity in Romans 1:26–27, 1 Corinthians 6:9, 1 Timothy 1:10 and Jude 7. These texts take a strongly negative view of both female and male same-sex sexual activity (Romans 1:26–27, 1 Timothy 1:10), of both passive and active male same-sex activity (1 Corinthians 6:9) and of homosexual lust (Jude 7). None of these texts, however, refers specifically to pederasty in the way that, for instance, the first century Jewish writer Philo of

---

[11] Boswell, *Christianity, Social Tolerance, and Homosexuality*, p. 28.
[12] See James Moulton and George Milligan, 'porneia' in *The Vocabulary of the Greek New Testament Illustrated from the Papyri and Other Non-Literary Sources* (Grand Rapids: Eerdmans, 1980); H. Reisser, 'Porneuō' in Colin Brown (ed.), *The New International Dictionary of the New Testament Theology* (Grand Rapids: Zondervan, 1975) 1:499; and John Nolland, 'Sexual Ethics and the Jesus of the Gospels', *Anvil*, Vol 26:1, 2009, pp. 21–30.

Alexandria does. The specific vocabulary used to describe pederasty is not used in these texts.[13]

In Romans 1:27 Paul's use of the 'males' is not, as Dr Tallon suggests, a reference to pederasty. Rather, like the reference to 'females' in the previous verse, it is an intertextual reference back to Genesis 1:26–28. What Paul is saying is that same-sex sexual relations are an example of the males and females created by God to be his image bearers acting in a way that both nature and Scripture show is contrary to the way they were created to act. Human beings were created by God to have sexual intercourse within marriage with the members of the opposite sex and by this means to 'be fruitful and multiply.' Same-sex sex involves a turning away from this calling.[14]

The reasons why the New Testament takes a negative view of same-sex sexual relationships

Thirdly, the theological reasons why the New Testament rejects same-sex sexual activity apply to *all* forms of such activity (in both the ancient world and today) and not just to pederasty. The criteria applied in the New Testament to sexual relationships are whether such relationships are in accordance with the order of things established by God at creation (as recorded in Genesis 1 and 2) and whether they are in accordance with the law God subsequently gave to Israel as a reflection of that order.

The reason the New Testament takes a negative view of all same-sex sexual relationships is that they fail on both counts. They go against the created order put in place by God (Romans 1:26–27) and they are contrary to the Ten Commandments and the teaching of Leviticus 18 and 20 (1 Corinthians 6:9–11, 1

---

[13] For an overview of the interpretation of these texts see Martin Davie, *Studies on the Bible and same-sex relationships since 2003* (Malton: Gilead Books/CEEC, 2015).

[14] For the intertextual echoes of Genesis 1 in Romans 1 see Robert Gagnon, *The Bible and Homosexual Practice* (Nashville: Abingdon Press, 2001), pp. 289–293; and Tom Wright, *Paul for Everyone: Romans Part 1, Chapters 1–8* (London: SPCK: 2004), pp. 20–24.

Timothy 1:10). For the New Testament writers, therefore, the question of whether or not a same-sex sexual relationship is a committed and loving one is theologically irrelevant, in the same way it would be in the case of an incestuous or adulterous relationship. For them, all such relationships are inherently wrong in all circumstances by dint of the very fact that they involve sexual activity between those of the same sex.

Conclusion

As we have seen, homosexuality means sexual activity between two persons of the same sex. Such activity existed in New Testament times just as it does today, and, just like today, it existed in a variety of forms. We can therefore rightly say that homosexuality existed in New Testament times.

What we can equally rightly say is that all forms of homosexuality are both referred to and rejected by the writers of the New Testament, both implicitly in their references to *porneia* and explicitly in their specific references to particular forms of homosexual activity.

Therefore, the answer to the question, 'Does the Bible Really Say...Anything at All about Homosexuality as we Understand it Today?' is 'Yes, it does. It says that homosexual practice is wrong. It is against creation and the law of God.'

2. The Bible and Extra-Marital Sex

The argument of Dr Warner

In the second in the 'Does the Bible Really Say...?' series, Dr Meg Warner considers the topic 'Does the Bible Really Say...that Sex Outside of Marriage is Wrong?'[1]

Dr Warner acknowledges that:

> the overwhelming impression of the various biblical references and allusions to sex outside marriage is negative. Extra-marital sex tends to be viewed in biblical texts as 'A Very Bad Thing'. One thinks, for example, of the professed view of Paul 'that it is better to be married than to burn' (1 Cor 7:9).[2]

However, she then goes on to argue that:

> In order to know whether, or how, the Bible's references and allusions to extra-marital sex ought to shape our conduct today, however, we need to look more closely.[3]

In order to take a closer look at the Bible's teaching she turns to the laws on sexual conduct in Deuteronomy 22:13–29 which she says are the 'foundation for biblical views on this subject'.[4] She summarises the contents of these verses as follows:

---

[1] Dr Meg Warner, 'Does the Bible Really Say...that Sex Outside Marriage is Wrong?', 23 May 2019, at https://viamedia.news/2019/05/23/does-the-bible-really-say-that-sex-outside-marriage-is-wrong/ (accessed 14 April 2020).
[2] Warner, 'Does the Bible Really Say...that Sex Outside Marriage is Wrong?'.
[3] Warner, 'Does the Bible Really Say...that Sex Outside Marriage is Wrong?'.
[4] Warner, 'Does the Bible Really Say...that Sex Outside Marriage is Wrong?'.

a single woman, living in the home of her father, should not have sex (so that she can present herself to her husband as a virgin – Deut 22:13–21), an engaged woman should not engage in consensual sex (Deut 22:23–29), and a married woman who has sex with someone other than her husband should die (Deut 22:22). Meanwhile, a man who has forced sex with a single woman will be required to pay a fee to her father, marry the girl and never divorce her (Deut 22:28–29), a man who has sex with an engaged woman should be put to death (Deut 22:23–27), and a man who has sex with another man's wife should be put to death (Deut 22:22).[1]

While accepting that these provisions in Deuteronomy 22 'could be viewed as a code that forbids sex outside of marriage', Dr Warner cautions against the simple assumption that what is said in these verses 'represents God's will for us today'.[2]

This is because underlying what is said in these verses is the idea of women as property. In Dr Warner's words:

Women were, in a very real sense, regarded as the property of the men to whom they 'belonged' – usually their fathers or husbands. In general, a woman was valuable to the man to whom she belonged, unless she failed to marry, in which case she became a burden. Marriage was in part a financial transaction, in which a girl's father looked to receive a 'marriage gift' or mohar from her suitor. A father owned not only his daughter, but also her sexuality, and virginity was

---

[1] Warner, 'Does the Bible Really Say...that Sex Outside Marriage is Wrong?'.
[2] Warner, 'Does the Bible Really Say...that Sex Outside Marriage is Wrong?'.

considered essential to what a woman brought to her marriage.[3]

According to Dr Warner this fact should lead the church to re-consider whether it should reject sex outside marriage for two reasons.

First, according to Dr Warner, the ideas reflected in Deuteronomy 22 are now outdated:

> We no longer, in the West, consider women to be the property of men, and while marriage may still be a family concern, it is no longer essentially a financial transaction. The principles set out in Deuteronomy 22 are no longer needed to ensure protection from shame and financial loss. Further, if we were all familiar with Deuteronomy 22, and understood the social values that it upheld, we would likely be appalled, and perhaps choose to boycott behavioural patterns based upon those social values, rather than to compel people to follow them.[4]

Secondly:

> those social values are not clearly of themselves inherently biblical. The code in Deuteronomy adopts prevalent community standards and attitudes, and makes special rules and provisions for Israelites. Today's prevalent community standards and attitudes are vastly different. The special rules and provisions put in place for ancient Israelites may not be helpful, and may even be harmful, in our context.[5]

---

[3] Warner, 'Does the Bible Really Say...that Sex Outside Marriage is Wrong?'.
[4] Warner, 'Does the Bible Really Say...that Sex Outside Marriage is Wrong?'.
[5] Warner, 'Does the Bible Really Say...that Sex Outside Marriage is Wrong?'.

Assessing this argument

What should we make of this argument? The answer is that we should reject it for two reasons.

First, there is nothing to suggest that what underlies the laws about sexual conduct in Deuteronomy 22:13–29 is a belief that a woman is the property of her father or her husband.

This is something that is not said anywhere in Deuteronomy 22, which means that the evidence for it has to lie somewhere else in the Old Testament. However, no such evidence exists. As Richard Davidson notes, the Old Testament nowhere suggests that women were regarded as property.[6]

Elsewhere in the Ancient New East, because wives and daughters were regarded as a man's property in the same way as his slaves or his oxen, a 'vicarious punishment' could be imposed in which 'a man was punished for a crime by having to give up his wife or daughter'. In the Old Testament, by contrast, where women are not regarded as property 'no such vicarious punishment is prescribed.' In similar fashion, he writes, because a wife was regarded as property, other Ancient Near Eastern law codes permit a husband to 'whip his wife, pluck out her hair, mutilate her ears, or strike her, with impunity', whereas 'no such permission is given to the husband in biblical law to punish his wife in any way.'[7]

As Davidson goes on to say:

> Far from being regarded as 'chattel,' according to the fifth commandment of the Decalogue and repeated commands throughout the Pentateuchal code, the wife/mother was to be given equal honour within the

---

[6] Richard Davidson, *Flame of Yahweh – Sexuality in the Old Testament* (Peabody: Hendrickson, 2007).
[7] Davidson, *Flame of Yahweh*, p. 250.

family circle (Exod 20:12; 21:15, 17, Lev 20:9; Deut 21:18–21; 27:16).[8]

If we ask why a wife or mother is to be given equal honour, the answer given in the Old Testament in the creation accounts in Genesis 1 and 2 is that it is because both women and men share the same humanity (Genesis 2:23) and as such have equal status as those created in God's image and likeness (Genesis 1:26–27). Eve is the equal human partner of Adam.

It is sometimes suggested that the tenth commandment of the Decalogue sees a wife as property alongside his manservant, his maidservant, or his ox, or his ass, or anything that is his neighbour's (Exodus 20:17). However, as John Otwell has pointed out, in fact the wife is not listed here as property, but simply as the first-named member of a household. This point is made clear in the parallel version of the commandment in Deuteronomy 5:21 where the wife is the subject of an entirely separate clause.[9]

As we have seen, Dr Warner argues that the Old Testament concept of the *mohar* paid by the bridegroom to the bride's father (Genesis 34:12, Exodus 22:17, 1 Samuel 18:25) indicates that marriage was viewed as a 'financial transaction' in which the husband purchased his wife from her father. However, as Roland De Vaux explains, this is not the case:

> This obligation to pay a sum of money, or its equivalent, to the girl's family obviously gives the Israelite marriage the outward appearance of a purchase. But the mohar seems not to be so much the price paid for the woman as a compensation given to the family, and, in spite of the apparent resemblance, in law this is a different consideration. The future

---

[8] Davidson, *Flame of Yahweh,* p. 250.
[9] John Otwell, *And Sarah Laughed: The Status of Women in the Old Testament* (Philadelphia: Westminster, 1977), p. 76.

husband thereby acquires a right over the woman, but the woman herself is not bought and sold.[10]

The reason compensation would be payable would be that a woman's labour would have economic value for her family and the loss of this would need to be made good. It would be paid to her father – as the representative of her family, not because he owned her.

It should also be noted that it appears that the *mohar* was held in trust with any added value belonging to the father and the family he represented, but with the capital reverting to the daughter on his death, or if she was reduced to poverty by the death of her husband. This explains the complaint by Rachel and Leah in Genesis 31:15 that Laban 'has been using up the money given for us.' [11] This too makes it clear that the *mohar* was not a payment to his father for his property.

Secondly, Dr Warner is mistaken when she declares that the case law in Deuteronomy 22 is 'the foundation for biblical views on this subject.'[12]

If what she means by this is that, historically, this was the first piece of biblical writing on the subject of sexual misconduct that then led to all the others, then there appears to be no evidence that this the case (and none is offered by Dr Warner).

If what she means is that within the Canon of Scripture this chapter is the definitive explanation of why sex outside marriage is to be rejected, then she is equally wrong. In the biblical Canon, the laws in Deuteronomy 22:13–29 are an amplification of the seventh commandment ('You shall not commit adultery') as recorded in Exodus 20:14 and Deuteronomy 5:18) which in turn reflects God's creation of

---

[10] Roland De Vaux, *Ancient Israel: Its life and institutions* (London: Darton, Longman and Todd, 1988), p. 27.

[11] De Vaux, *Ancient Israel*, p. 27.

[12] Warner, 'Does the Bible Really Say...that Sex Outside Marriage is Wrong?'.

marriage as a sexually exclusive relationship between one man and one woman in Genesis 2:24. Furthermore, if we move to the New Testament, the apostle Paul tells us that the marital relationship established in Genesis 2:24 is itself based on something more fundamental, namely the eternal relationship between Christ and his church to which human marriage points (Ephesians 5:32).

Why are the various forms of sexual conduct described in Deuteronomy 22:13–29 wrong? Because they are all forms of sex outside marriage which are all covered by the general prohibition of adultery in the Decalogue. Why does the Decalogue prohibit adultery? Because God established marriage as an exclusive sexual relationship pointing to the exclusive and permanent relationship between Christ and his people.

What all this in turn means is that the biblical rejection of all forms of sex outside marriage, like the biblical insistence on the equal dignity of men and women, is not, as Dr Warner suggests, simply a reflection of cultural attitudes commonly held across the ancient world. Instead, it is based on a view of God's creation of the world and of God's relationship with his people that is unique to the Scriptures of the Old and New Testaments.

A final point made by Dr Warner that we need to consider is her claim that:

> both Exodus and Deuteronomy make provision for the family of a single woman who is sexually assaulted to be married off to her assailant. At the time of writing these provisions functioned pastorally. Today, in the West at least, they would be considered abusive.[13]

---

[13] Warner, 'Does the Bible Really Say...that Sex Outside Marriage is Wrong?'.

The texts she is referring to are Exodus 22:16–17 and Deuteronomy 22:28–29 and the problem with her reading of them is twofold.

First, Exodus 22:16 talks about 'seduction' not assault and the specific Hebrew word *tapas* used to describe the sexual activity in Deuteronomy 22:28 plus its statement that 'they' (and not just 'he') are caught in the act likewise seem to indicate 'that the woman had acquiesced and was a willing partner in the sexual encounter.'[14]

Secondly, it is not a case of the woman alone being 'married off'. Both the man and the woman have to marry. What the texts imply is that if an unmarried couple decide to have sex then they have to accept the consequences of their action (except in the case where the man is completely unsuitable for some reason in which case the girl's father has the right to forbid the marriage – Exodus 22:17).

Conclusion

What we have seen is that Dr Warner's argument is misleading in several respects.

- It is not the case that Deuteronomy 22:13–29 is the foundation for the biblical rejection of sex outside marriage

- It is not the case that what is said in these verses depends on the idea that a woman is the property of her father or her husband

- It is not the case that these verses simply echo the ideas of the surrounding culture

---

[14] Davidson, *Flame of Yahweh*, p. 359. See also Moshe Weinfeld, *Deuteronomy and the Deuteronomic School* (Winona Lake: Eisenbrauns, 1992) p. 286; and Katie McCoy, 'Did Old Testament Law Force a Woman to Marry Her Rapist?', The Council on Biblical Manhood and Womanhood, 5 March 2018, https://cbmw.org/topics/sex/did-old-testament-law-force-a-woman-to-marry-her-rapist/ (accessed 14 April 2020).

- It is not the case that Exodus 22:16–17 and Deuteronomy 22:28–29 are about a woman being married off to someone who has sexually assaulted her

In addition, Dr Warner has failed to acknowledge the way in which the actual foundation for biblical thinking about sexual ethics is the creation narrative in Geneses 1 and 2 and what the apostle Paul says in Ephesians 5:32 about marriage being a reflection of Christ's relationship with his church.

For all these reasons, her article does not make out a persuasive case for the church to reconsider its traditional view that faithful Christian discipleship requires sexual abstinence outside marriage and sexual fidelity within it.

This does not mean that Christians today need to adopt the specific laws laid down in Deuteronomy 22. As Article VI of the Thirty-Nine Articles says, is it not the case that the 'civil precepts' contained in the Old Testament 'ought of necessity to be received in any commonwealth'.[15] What it does means, as Oliver O'Donovan writes, is that as Christians we need to learn to see within this law (as within the Old Testament law as a whole) 'a revelation of created order and the good to which all men are called, a "moral law" by which every human being is claimed and which belongs fundamentally to men's welfare.'[16]

In this case the 'moral law' in question is that sex belongs exclusively within (heterosexual) marriage.

---

[15] Article VI *Thirty-Nine Articles*, 1571.
[16] Oliver O'Donovan, *On the Thirty-Nine Articles* (Exeter: Paternoster, 1986), p. 64.

3. The Clarity of the Bible with Regard to Marriage

In the third in the 'Does the Bible Really Say...?' series, Professor Martyn Percy addresses the question, 'Does the Bible Really...Give us a Clear Definition of Marriage?'[1]

Given that this is the question that his article is supposed to be addressing, it is unfortunate that he never gets around to answering it. In his article, he explains why he thinks we should not adopt a 'fundamentalistic' approach to the Bible, highlights the problems, as he sees them, of adhering to a traditional 'biblical' view of marriage in practice, and stresses that a loving marriage is a 'sacramental token of love'.[2] However, none of this answers the question of whether the Bible gives us a clear definition of marriage.

The nearest Professor Percy gets to answering this question is when he claims, without any further evidence or explanation, that 'Scripture does not lay down one pattern of marriage' and that 'The Bible offers several patterns of marriage'.[3]

What are we to make of this claim that the Bible does not offer us one pattern of marriage, but several?

In one of my favourite Christian novels, the hero declares 'the good stuff is in the details.'[4] In terms of our approach to the Bible what this means is that we cannot rest content with the

---

[1] Martyn Percy, 'Does the Bible Really...Give Us a Clear Definition of Marriage?', 31 May 2019, at https://viamedia.news/2019/05/31/does-the-bible-really-give-us-a-clear-definition-of-marriage/ (accessed 14 April 2020).

[2] Percy, 'Does the Bible Really...Give Us a Clear Definition of Marriage?'.

[3] Percy, 'Does the Bible Really...Give Us a Clear Definition of Marriage?'.

[4] Dee Henderson, *The Guardian* (Carol Stream: Tyndale, 2005), p.86.

sort of unverified generalisations that Professor Percy offers us in his article. Rather, we have to consider the details of what the Bible says on any given topic. If we do this in relation to marriage, we discover that what Professor Percy says is misleading for a number of reasons.

First, the Bible restricts what it says about marriage to marriage between people of the opposite sex. It is simply not the case that there are two patterns of marriage in Scripture, one heterosexual and the other homosexual. As Michael Brown writes, 'Every single reference to marriage in the entire Bible speaks of heterosexual unions, without exception, to the point that a Hebrew idiom for marriage is for a man "to take a wife".'[1]

Secondly, the Bible is also silent about polyandry. There are no examples in the Bible of a woman with multiple husbands.

Thirdly, what this means is that the only two patterns of marriage to which the Bible does refer are heterosexual polygyny (one man with multiple wives) and heterosexual monogamy.

If we look at polygyny first of all, what we find is that there are no references to polygynous marriages in the New Testament. All the references to marriage in the New Testament, without exception, are references to the marriage of one man with one woman.

There is polygyny in the Old Testament. However, it is very rare. As Richard Davidson notes: 'In the OT there are thirty-three reasonably clear historical cases of polygamy out of approximately three thousand men recorded in the scriptural record.'[2]

These rare cases of polygyny are almost entirely restricted to the period of the Patriarchs and to the judges and kings of pre-

---

[1] Michael Brown, *Can you be Gay and Christian?* (Lake Mary: Front Line, 2014) p. 87.
[2] Davidson, *Flame of Yahweh*, p. 210. In context what he means by 'polygamy' is specifically polygyny.

exilic Israel. There is only one instance of an ordinary Israelite being in a polygynous marriage (Elkanah in 1 Samuel 1:2).

Furthermore, when polygyny is referred to it is always referred to negatively:

- It is something engaged in by people who have turned away from God, as in the cases of Gideon in Judges 8:30 and Solomon in 1 Kings 11:1–8. Conversely, when people turn back to God, as in the case of Jacob and David (Genesis 32:22-32, 2 Samuel 15:30), they also turn back to monogamy.

- It something that is forbidden to both the people of Israel in general, and specifically to their kings, by God's law in Leviticus 18:18 (where 'sister' means another woman rather than someone with the same parents) and Deuteronomy 17:17.

- It is something that is depicted as leading to family conflict, as in the cases of the families of Jacob in Genesis 29:15–30: 24, Elkanah in 1 Samuel 1:3–8 and David in 1 Samuel 16–1 Kings 2.

- It has its origins after the Fall. In Genesis 4:17–24, we have a genealogy of the descendants of Cain. In this genealogy, the seventh and concluding figure in whom the descent into sin reaches its climax is Lamech, who is described not once, but three times, as having two wives (Genesis 4:19, 23a, 23b). In this account, Lamech's sinfulness is demonstrated not only by the fact that he is addicted to a life of violence and revenge, but that he has departed from the monogamous form of marriage established by God at creation (a point highlighted by the three references to his polygyny).[3]

---

[3] For a detailed study of polygyny in the Old Testament, with copious references to other studies, see Davidson, *Flame of Yahweh*, Chapter 5.

If we ask how we know that monogamy has been established by God at creation, the answer is that we are told this in the creation story in Genesis 2 which fills out what is said about God's creation of human beings as male and female in Genesis 1:26–28. In Genesis 2, God creates the woman, Eve, as the suitable partner for the man, Adam, and brings them together (Genesis 2:18–23). The narrator then goes on to explain that, by doing this, God established a pattern for all subsequent marriages: 'Therefore a man leaves his father and mother and cleaves to his wife, and they become one flesh' (Genesis 2:24).

What we have here is a normative pattern for marriage, upheld by Jesus himself in the Gospels (Matthew 19:3–6, Mark 10:2–9), that sees marriage as a freely chosen, permanent and exclusive sexual relationship that is between one man and one woman, and is outside of the immediate family circle. Moreover, as Genesis goes on to make clear through the subsequent story of Adam and Eve (Genesis 4:1, 2, 25, 5:3), it is through marriage that the divine command to 'be fruitful and multiply' in Genesis 1:28 is to find fulfilment.

The reason that the New Testament is silent about polygyny (as about polyandry and same-sex marriage) is that it holds that Christians are called to live with within the pattern of marriage thus established by God at creation and, by so doing, reflect the eternal marriage between Christ and his church (Ephesians 5:21–33).

The answer to the question posed in Professor Percy's article is thus that the Bible really does give us a clear definition of marriage. Marriage is what God says it is in Genesis 2. The Church of England is thus justified in saying that:

> marriage is in its nature a union permanent and lifelong, for better for worse, till death them do part, of one man with one woman, to the exclusion of all others on either side, for the procreation and nurture of children, for the hallowing and right direction of the natural instincts and affections, and for the mutual

society, help and comfort which the one ought to have
of the other, both in prosperity and adversity.[4]

This statement reflects the teaching of Scripture and so for the
Church of England to depart from it either by changing its
theology or its practice would mean departing from what God
has laid down – something which it is not authorised to do.

---

[4] Canon B30, 'Of Holy Matrimony' The Canons of the Church of
England, 7th ed. (London: Church House Publishing, 2016).

4. The Bible and 'Same-Sex Love'

In the fourth in the 'Does the Bible Really Say...?' series, the former Bishop of Bolton, David Gillett, addresses the issue of whether the Bible really views same-sex love as wrong.[1]

Bishop Gillett's argument

The starting point for his article is his conviction that 'unlike in the ancient Near East, we understand that God creates us with different sexual orientations.'[2] As a consequence, he says, 'we now approach the Bible with a broader and different set of questions than believers and scholars of former ages.'[3]

Bishop Gillett then suggests that we should not begin looking at what the Bible says about same-sex love by looking at those '6 or so verses in the Bible where certain same-sex activities are forbidden in differing cultures, contexts and religious situations', in the same way that we would not begin a study of heterosexual love by looking at those forms of sexual activity prohibited by the Bible.[4]

In line with this approach, he begins instead by looking at the biblical accounts of Ruth and Naomi and David and Jonathan. What these accounts show, he writes, 'is a quality of commitment and relationship which is part of our God-given humanity.'[5]

He next goes on to argue that in spite of the fact that the church has frequently surrounded sexual activity with 'prohibitions,

---

[1] David Gillett, 'Does the Bible Really Say that...Same-Sex Love is Wrong?', 6 June 2019, at https://viamedia.news/2019/06/06/does-the-bible-really-say-that-same-sex-love-is-wrong/ (accessed 14 April 2020).

[2] Gillett, 'Does the Bible Really Say that...Same-Sex Love is Wrong?'.

[3] Gillett, 'Does the Bible Really Say that...Same-Sex Love is Wrong?'.

[4] Gillett, 'Does the Bible Really Say that...Same-Sex Love is Wrong?'.

[5] Gillett, 'Does the Bible Really Say that...Same-Sex Love is Wrong?'.

cautions and caveats', it is nonetheless the case that 'sexual relationship is part of the very essence of God's good gifts to the whole of humanity.'[1]

Because this so, he contends we should pose a fresh question to the creation narrative in Genesis 2 which is 'How will a gay Adam whom God has made discover the partner "fit for him"?'[2] The answer, Bishop Gillett says, is that:

> He will naturally discover the answer for a wholesome, enjoyable and intimate sexual relationship with another man. It is a denial of God's creative purposes to prohibit sexual expression to same-sex couples in their relationship while encouraging it between two of the opposite sex, as all are equally part of God's good creation.[3]

Understanding that some people are created as gay also means, he argues, that we now need to read passages such as Romans 1:26–27 in a new way. In Romans 1, he says, Paul is not:

> issuing an apostolic evaluation of the permanent faithful same-sex loving relationships which we see with many of our LGBT+ friends. Rather, he is condemning salacious sexual experimentation, domination of slaves or minors, promiscuity and pagan cultic practices and prostitution.[4]

Finally, Bishop Gillett concludes his article by appealing to three New Testament texts which he thinks show how the Gospel calls Christians to accept all people equally, regardless of their sexuality.

The first text is Acts 10:15, 'What God has called clean, you must not call profane.'(NTE) In this verse, according to Bishop

---

[1] Gillett, 'Does the Bible Really Say that...Same-Sex Love is Wrong?'.
[2] Gillett, 'Does the Bible Really Say that...Same-Sex Love is Wrong?'.
[3] Gillett, 'Does the Bible Really Say that...Same-Sex Love is Wrong?'.
[4] Gillett, 'Does the Bible Really Say that...Same-Sex Love is Wrong?'.

Gillett, Peter 'sees that what God creates as clean and acceptable must not be categorised as unclean or unacceptable, even if the law or religious tradition claims otherwise.'⁵ For us this means that:

> we must abandon the unjust and unjustifiable categorization of LGBT+ people and their relationships as somehow less than fully wholesome. They are an equal part of the diversity of God's good creation. Same-sex love is as natural, good and wholesome for gay and lesbian people as are male-female sexual relationships for the rest of us.⁶

The second text is Ephesians 2:14 (NRSVA): 'For he is our peace; in his flesh he has made both groups into one and has broken down the dividing wall, that is, the hostility between us'. Gillett says that what this tells us is that 'the loving action of God in Christ' breaks down the division between those who are gay and those who are straight and so 'For us to seek to build such walls and treat others as "outsiders" is to put the Gospel into reverse.'⁷

The third text is Galatians 3:28 (NRSVA): 'There is no longer Jew or Greek, there is no longer slave or free, there is no longer male or female; for all of you are one in Christ Jesus.' In this verse, according to Gillett, Paul:

> makes clear that all the inherited divisions within humanity which have marred our communities and given power to one group over another have no place within the community redeemed by Christ.⁸

This means that:

---

⁵ Gillett, 'Does the Bible Really Say that...Same-Sex Love is Wrong?'.
⁶ Gillett, 'Does the Bible Really Say that...Same-Sex Love is Wrong?'.
⁷ Gillett, 'Does the Bible Really Say that...Same-Sex Love is Wrong?'.
⁸ Gillett, 'Does the Bible Really Say that...Same-Sex Love is Wrong?'.

> *The Church, if it is true to its very essence, must be at*
> *the forefront of treating LGBT+ people and their*
> *relationships with total equality. Where this is denied,*
> *the Gospel itself is diminished and robbed of its*
> *power, making the good news 'bad news' for many.*[9]

According to Bishop Gillett, the message of 'full acceptance
and inclusion' contained in these three verses,

> affirms the value of same-sex couples. It forms the
> basis of how we can support and celebrate same-sex
> relations and equal marriage as an outworking of
> God's will for the whole of his creation in all its
> wonderful diversity.
>
> It is something which, without fear of disregarding
> the bible's authority within the Church, we can
> proclaim as just, equitable and worthy of celebration![10]

What are we to make of this argument?

The first issue raised by Bishop Gillett's argument is on what
basis he thinks we now know that some people are created by
God for a sexual relationship with those of the same sex as
themselves. There are two possible ways we might know this,
through what we can observe of the way God has made the
world and through God's revelation of his creative intention in
the Bible.

If we begin with what we can learn from the way God has made
the world, we discover that God has made human beings in a
particular way. To quote the American writer Christopher
Tollefsen:

> ... our identity as animal organisms is the foundation
> of our existence as selves. But fundamental to our
> existence as this animal is our sex. We are male or

---

[9] Gillett, 'Does the Bible Really Say that...Same-Sex Love is Wrong?'.
[10] Gillett, 'Does the Bible Really Say that...Same-Sex Love is Wrong?'.

female organisms in virtue of having a root capacity for reproductive function, even when that capacity is immature or damaged. In human beings, as is the case with many other organisms, that function is one to be performed jointly with another human being; unlike the digestive function, no individual human being suffices for its performance.

Accordingly, reproductive function in human beings is distributed across the two sexes, which are identified by their having the root capacity for one or the other of the two general structural and behavioural patterns involved in human reproduction. In male humans, this capacity is constituted by the structures necessary for the production of male gametes and the performance of the male sex act, insemination. In females, the capacity is constituted by the structures necessary for the production of oocytes and the performance of the female sex act, the reception of semen in a manner disposed to conception.[11]

What this means is that human beings are designed by their creator to have sexual intercourse with members of the opposite sex. This is how God has created human beings to be. That is also why Paul says in Romans 1:26–27 that sexual relations between two people of the same sex are 'unnatural.' The point that Paul is making is that the very structure of the human body shows that men were designed by God to have sex with women and vice versa. To have same-sex sex is thus to disregard what the created order teaches us about the will of God for his human creatures in the same way that idolatry

---

[11] Christopher O. Tollefsen, 'Sex Identity,' Public Discourse, 13 July 2015, https://www.thepublicdiscourse.com/2015/07/15306/ (accessed 14 April 2020).

involves disregarding what the created order teaches us about God's nature and existence.[12]

The biblical accounts of creation in Genesis 1 and 2 affirm and supplement the witness of the created order. Genesis 1 declares that God has created human beings in his image and likeness as male and female and has given them the mandate to be fruitful and multiply (Genesis 1:26–28). Genesis 2 likewise declares that the proper partner for the male Adam is the female Eve and that God has ordained marriage between a man and a woman as the proper context for sexual union and hence the means by which the mandate to have offspring is meant to be fulfilled (Genesis 2:18–24).

Bishop Gillett's suggestion that we can read Genesis 2 as saying that the proper sexual partner for a 'gay Adam' is another man involves setting aside the very point that Genesis 2 is making, which is that by God's design the proper sexual partner for a man is a woman.

What all this means is that neither nature nor Scripture support Bishop Gillett's contention that God has created some people to have sexual intercourse with members of their own sex. It follows that we therefore cannot say that this is something that we now know.

Moving on to the second point that the bishop makes, the biblical stories of Ruth and Naomi and David and Jonathan do indeed show qualities of 'commitment and relationship' which are an important part of our God-given humanity. However, what neither story suggests is that such commitment and relationship can find its legitimate expression in a same-sex sexual relationship. Neither story hints at any such thing.

It is true that both stories show that love between two people of the same sex is morally acceptable, but love and sex are not the

---

[12] For this point see Gagnon, *The Bible and Homosexual Practice*, pp. 254–270.

same thing. The stories affirm same-sex love, but they do not affirm same-sex sex.

The bishop's third point, that we need to read Romans 1 in a new way, is equally misleading. There is nothing in what Paul says in Romans 1:26–27 that suggests that Paul is only rejecting particular forms of same-sex sexual activity. As we have already noted, the point that Paul is making is that *all* forms of male-male and female-female sexual intercourse are wrong because they go against the way God created human beings to be. There can be no exceptions because there are no human beings whom God has created in a different way.

This brings us on to the bishop's fourth point, the claim that we must regard same-sex sexual relationships as 'wholesome' because they are 'an equal part of the diversity of God's good creation.'[13] There is nothing in Scripture to support this claim and, as we have seen, it is also unsupported by the witness of nature.

The bishop's final point is that what is said about the inclusive nature of the Gospel in Ephesians 2:14 and Galatians 3:28 means that the church must accept gay and lesbian people and their relationships. The problem with this part of his argument is that it confuses acceptance of all types of people with acceptance of all forms of behaviour. The New Testament is clear that all types of people – whatever their race, sex, or social standing – are to be welcomed into the church on the basis of faith in Jesus Christ (this is the point that Paul is making in Galatians 3:28). However, it is equally clear that becoming part of the church brings with it an obligation to abandon certain forms of behaviour.

In his letter to the Ephesians, for example, Paul insists that Gentiles are part of the church just as much as Jews, but he also tells his readers that they must no longer engage in Gentile forms of behaviour:

---

[13] Gillett, 'Does the Bible Really Say that...Same-Sex Love is Wrong?'.

Now this I affirm and testify in the Lord, that you must no longer live as the Gentiles do, in the futility of their minds; they are darkened in their understanding, alienated from the life of God because of the ignorance that is in them, due to their hardness of heart; they have become callous and have given themselves up to licentiousness, greedy to practice every kind of uncleanness. You did not so learn Christ! – assuming that you have heard about him and were taught in him, as the truth is in Jesus. Put off your old nature which belongs to your former manner of life and is corrupt through deceitful lusts, and be renewed in the spirit of your minds, and put on the new nature, created after the likeness of God in true righteousness and holiness (Ephesians 4:17–24, RSV).

Among the forms of behaviour which are thus off limits for Christians are all forms of same-sex sexual activity.

The New Testament builds on the condemnation of male homosexual activity in the Old Testament law (Leviticus 18:22, 20:13) by declaring that both male and female same-sex relationships are symptoms of the way human beings have turned away from God (Romans 1:26–27). They are one of the sinful ways of life from which God has rescued Christians (1 Corinthians 6:9–11). They are examples of conduct which is contrary to 'sound doctrine' and the 'glorious gospel' (1 Timothy 1:10–11). In addition, the New Testament also includes same-sex sexual activity when it says that Christians must avoid all forms of *porneia* or sexual immorality (see for instance Mark 7:21, Galatians 5:19, 1 Thessalonians 4:3 and Hebrews 13:4).

What this means is that while Christians must welcome both those with same-sex attraction and those in same-sex relationships, they also have a duty to make it crystal clear that all forms of same-sex sexual activity, like all forms of sexual activity outside heterosexual marriage, are contrary to the will of God.

Conclusion

We have to say, therefore, that none of the points put forward by Bishop Gillett in his article are persuasive.

We do not now know that God created some people to be gay or lesbian. We cannot rightly read Genesis 2, or the stories of Ruth and Naomi and David and Jonathan, as supporting same-sex sexual relationships. Romans 1:26–27 sees all forms of same-sex sex as contrary to the way God created human beings to be and we have no basis for saying that same-sex sexual relationships are regarded by God as 'wholesome'. Finally, while Christians must welcome all people, the New Testament is clear that there are certain forms of behaviour that are off limits for those in the church and that this includes same-sex sex.

5. Were the Sodomites Sodomites?

The traditional view of the story of Sodom

In the Bible, the story of the destruction of the cities of Sodom and Gomorrah is consistently depicted as an example of the judgement of God upon human sinfulness. The people of Sodom 'were wicked, great sinners against the Lord' (Genesis 13:13 ,) and God eventually wiped them and the neighbouring cities from the face of the earth.

The story of the final destruction of these cities is told in Genesis 19:1–29 and the traditional Christian reading of this story is that the final act of sinfulness by the men of Sodom was an attempt to have homosexual sex with the two male visitors staying in Lot's house. On the basis of this reading of the story, 'sodomite' has become a traditional term for those who engage in same-sex sexual activity (particularly male-male sexual activity) and Genesis 19 has become one of the standard proof texts used to show that such activity is sinful.

Dr Warner's three alternative readings

In response to this, those theologians who have sought to argue that same-sex sexual activity ought not to be regarded as sinful have sought to challenge the traditional reading of Genesis 19. In the fifth of the 'Does the Bible Really Say...?' series, Dr Meg Warner follows this revisionist approach by arguing that the Bible doesn't really tell us that the Sodomites were sodomites.[1]

In her paper, she puts forward three alternative readings of the Sodom story.

---

[1] Meg Warner, 'Does the Bible Really Say...that Sodomites were sodomites?', 13 June 2019 at
https://viamedia.news/2019/06/13/does-the-bible-really-say-that-sodomites-were-sodomites/ (accessed 14 April 2020).

The story of Sodom is about rape

First, she argues that the story of Sodom is irrelevant to the issue of consensual, loving same-sex relationships:

> Genesis 19 may be many things, but it is NOT evidence about God's attitude towards loving, sexual relationships between men (or women, for that matter). It tells a story in which a group of men apparently threaten to pack-rape some other men (who are actually angels), but it has nothing to say about the kind of same-sex relationships that are currently getting the churches so het-up.[1]

The story of Sodom is about using sex to become divine

Secondly, she suggests that the intended sin of the men of Sodom may actually have been the attempt to use sex to achieve divine status:

> Nowhere else in the book of Genesis is concern expressed about sex between men, but sexual activity between humans and divine beings is a pervasive theme. In Genesis 6 the wickedness (r') of humankind, manifesting itself in sexual congress between 'daughters of humans' and 'sons of God', so grieves God that God decides to blot out all humans and living things from the face of the earth. Interestingly, the same Hebrew root is used by Lot in Genesis 19:7, 'I beg you, my brothers, do not act so wickedly (r')' and by the narrator in Genesis 13:13, 'Now, the people of Sodom were wicked (r') ...'. This strikingly consistent use of the language of wickedness (r') supports an argument that, had the men of Sodom gone on to have sex with the visitors, their crime would not have been homosexuality but

---

[1] Warner, 'Does the Bible Really Say...that Sodomites were sodomites?'.

hubris—the pursuit of divinity by means of intercourse with divine beings.[2]

The story of Sodom is a story of misunderstanding

Thirdly (and this seems to be her preferred reading), Dr Warner suggests that the story can be read a story in which Lot misunderstands the request made by the Sodomites to 'know' his visitors:

> Interpreters of Genesis 19 today are increasingly likely to look past their gut-reactions to words such as 'Sodom' and 'Sodomite' and to scenarios of same-sex violence, and to focus instead on the literary and socio-political contexts of the text. They identify both Genesis 18 (Abraham's welcome of three strangers at Mamre) and 19 as stories about hospitality that reflect the hospitality codes of their time, recognising Genesis 18 as a story of hospitality to strangers in a non-urban context and Genesis 19 as a story about the particular challenges and tensions of offering hospitality in an urban setting. These challenges and tensions arise as a consequence of the risks inherent in inviting strangers to remain within city walls overnight. Issuing such invitations was the privilege of a city's male citizens. The conflict in Genesis 19 arises from the fact that Lot assumes this privilege for himself, as can be seen clearly in verse 9, in which the angry citizens of Sodom say, 'This fellow came here as an alien, and he would play the judge!'

> The men of Sodom aren't just feeling lustful on a slow Friday night. They are angry (and, to some extent, justifiably so) with Johnny-come-lately Lot for placing them and their women and children in danger by

---

[2] Warner, 'Does the Bible Really Say...that Sodomites were sodomites?'

inviting strangers to stay within the walls overnight. They want to 'know' (yd') who the visitors are, so that they can assess the level of threat. Lot, who doesn't 'get' all of this any more than some modern commentators (!), misunderstands the men's demands as sexual but is unwilling to allow strangers under his roof to be mistreated, and offers his virgin daughters in their place – thus responding to the 'comically grotesque' in-hospitality of the Sodomites with comically grotesque hospitality, unimaginable to today's readers in the West, but not unknown still in some parts of the world, and iconic in Lot's own context.[3]

The problems with Dr Warner's three readings

What are we to make of these three alternative readings?

If we take her preferred reading first of all, the first thing to note is that she has misinterpreted Genesis 19:9. The accusation that Lot is seeking to 'play the judge', even though he is an alien, refers not to his offering his two visitors hospitality, but to his request to the men of Sodom not to do harm to his visitors, 'only do nothing to these men, for they have come under the shelter of my roof' (19:8,). The conflict in Genesis 19 is thus not about Lot offering hospitality, but about his refusal to acquiesce to the demands of the crowd.

More fundamentally, however, this reading of the text depends on our knowing about the motives of the men of Sodom in a way that Lot does not. How do we know that Lot's belief that the men's demand is sexual is a misunderstanding? The text certainly does not say so.

Genesis has told us about the wickedness of Sodom in 13:13 and this point is reinforced in Genesis 18:20 where we are told that 'the outcry against Sodom and Gomorrah is great and their sin

---

[3] Warner, 'Does the Bible Really Say...that Sodomites were sodomites?'.

is very grave'. According to Genesis 18:21 the purpose of the visit of the two angels to Sodom is to give the cities one last chance by allowing God to assess the situation for himself; 'I will go down to see whether they have done altogether according to the outcry which has come to me; and if not I will know' ().

In this context, the purpose of the story in Genesis 19:1–11 is to show why the cities fail the test and are destroyed. The reason they fail the test (and why Sodom and Gomorrah are subsequently destroyed) is that the men of Sodom confirm the depravity of the inhabitants of the cities by seeking to act 'wickedly' (19:7) in wanting to 'know' Lot's visitors. The story thus only makes sense if the men of Sodom really are wanting to act in a wicked fashion. The idea that it is all one big misunderstanding simply doesn't fit the plot line of the narrative.

Even if we accept this point it still leaves open the question as to what the wickedness in question was. However, the following points make it clear that the wickedness consisted in the desire for homosexual sex.

- The juxtaposition of the use of the Hebrew verb *yada* ('know') in verses 5 and 8 indicates that the verb has the same meaning in both cases and since the meaning in verse 8 is clearly sexual, 'Behold, I have two daughters who have not known man', it follows that the meaning in the request in verse 5 'that we may know them' must be the same. The men of Sodom want to have sex with Lot's visitors.

- This reading of the text is reinforced by the fact that in Judges 19:22–26, a text which scholars generally agree is based on the Sodom story (and which is thus the first commentary on it), the verb *yada* is also used with a consistently sexual meaning.

- This reading of the text is further supported by the nature of Lot's counter offer to the men of Sodom, have sex with my two daughters instead of my two visitors, and by the double use of the specific term 'male' (*anse*) in 19:4 (itself an intertextual echo of the use of the term 'male' in the reference to the wickedness of Sodom in Genesis 13:13). Those who are proposing to act wickedly in Sodom are the male inhabitants of the city and the nature of their proposed wickedness is sex with Lot's (supposedly) male visitors.

- Finally, this reading of the text is supported by the fact noted by James De Young that in the literary structure of Genesis, the story of Sodom forms part of a trio of stories that sit between the promise of the birth of Isaac in Genesis 18:9–15 and its fulfilment in Genesis 21:1–7, the other two being the story of the incest of Lot and his daughters (Genesis 19:30–38) and the story of Abraham, Sarah and Abimelech (Genesis 20:1–18).[4] As De Young explains 'each episode relates sexual sin and its punishment ... The literary structure of the text demands a homosexual meaning for the sin of Sodom. Illicit sexual enjoyment or opportunism links all three episodes.'[5]

Moving on to Dr Warner's second suggestion, her idea that we can read Genesis 19 as being about the desire of the men of Sodom to use sex to attain divinity is problematic for a number of reasons.

First, it is simply not the case, as Dr Warner claims, that 'sexual activity between humans and divine beings' is a 'pervasive theme' in the book of Genesis.[6] There is only one text where such activity might possibly be referred to, namely Genesis 6:1–4, and even in this text it is much more probable that the 'sons

---

[4] James De Young, *Homosexuality: Contemporary Claims Examined in Light of the Bible and Other Ancient Literature and Law* (Grand Rapids: Kregel, 2000).

[5] De Young, *Homosexuality*, pp. 39–40.

[6] Warner, 'Does the Bible Really Say...that Sodomites were sodomites?'.

of God' are male human beings of the line of Seth rather than angels.[7]

Secondly, there is no indication in the text of Genesis 19 that the men of Sodom know that Lot's visitors are angels. Verse 5 tells us that the men of Sodom referred to them as 'men'. The reader of Genesis knows that the visitors are angels. The men of Sodom do not.

Thirdly, In Jude 7 the Greek words *sarkos heteras* (translated 'unnatural lust' in the RSV) literally mean 'a different kind of flesh.' What Jude 7 thus says is that the men of Sodom 'pursued a different kind of flesh' and some commentators have taken this to mean that they sought to have sex with angels. Dr Warner accepts this idea, but a more probable interpretation is that the 'different kind of flesh' they pursued was the flesh of other men rather than the flesh of women. In the words of Peter Davids in his commentary on Jude, 'it is more likely that Jude too is thinking of homosexual activity as the "different kind of flesh" (different not from themselves, but from the women they were supposed to desire).'[8]

This view is supported by:

- the fact that it would have been as obvious to Jude as to us that the men of Sodom did not know that Lot's visitors were angels

- the fact that there is no other Jewish or early Christian writing that supports the idea that the sin of Sodom and Gomorrah was a desire for sex with angels[9]

- the fact that the aorist tenses used in Jude 7 indicate that the judgement of God occurred when the inhabitants of

---

[7] For this point see Davidson, *Flame of Yahweh,* pp. 181–184.

[8] Peter Davids, *The Letters of 2 Peter and Jude* (Grand Rapids/Nottingham: Apollos, 2006), p. 53.

[9] The apocryphal Jewish text *The Testament of Naphtali* has been suggested as an example, but this is not the most likely reading of this text.

> Sodom, Gomorrah and the surrounding cities had already
> acted immorally and 'pursued a different kind of flesh', and
> this existing sexual immorality cannot have involved
> seeking sex with angels

If we turn to Dr Warner's first suggestion, which is that even if
the Sodom story is about sex, it is about rape rather than about
loving sexual relationships, the point to note is that, as Victor
Hamilton points out in his commentary on Genesis, Hebrew
has a vocabulary used to describe rape and this is not used in
Genesis 19:5.[10] All that this verse tells us, therefore, is that the
men of Sodom wanted to have sexual relations with Lot's
visitors. It does not limit what the men of Sodom were
contemplating to rape, even if the context suggests that this
may have been what the crowd had in mind.

The fact that the text leaves it at that and that it says nothing
about the motivation of the crowd, or whether they were
homosexual or bisexual, is theologically significant. In order to
make it clear that Sodom was a gravely sinful place, all that the
text has to say is that its male inhabitants sought to have sex
with other men. That in itself constitutes a wicked act (Genesis
19:6) which illustrates the more general wickedness for which
Sodom, Gomorrah, and two neighbouring cities are going to be
destroyed.

In Genesis 19, as in Judges 19, the desire for homosexual sex
is in itself evidence of the wider sinfulness of a society that has
turned from God and is therefore subject to God's judgement.
This is the same point that is made on an even wider canvas by
Paul in Romans 1:26–27.

Conclusion

What all this means is that none of the three alternative
readings of the story of Sodom proposed by Dr Warner are
persuasive. The best reading of Genesis 19:1–11 remains the

---

[10] Victor Hamilton, *The Book of Genesis: Chapters 18–50* (Grand
Rapids: Eerdmans, 1995), pp. 34–35.

traditional one that sees the Sodomites (and the inhabitants of the neighbouring cities) as people who engaged in same-sex sexual activity and were thus in the traditional sense sodomites.

Furthermore as Sam Allberry, who is himself same-sex attracted, notes, according to Jude 7:

> What happened at Sodom is clearly meant to be a cautionary tale. They are an example of facing God's judgment. Peter says much the same. Sodom and Gomorrah stand 'as an example of what is going to happen to the ungodly' (2 Peter 2:6). Jude makes it clear that their ungodliness involved sexual immorality. They were punished for sexual sin along with the other sins of which they were guilty. Their destruction serves as a warning: **God takes sexual sin very seriously.**[11]

Because God takes sexual sin very seriously, it follows that orthodox Christians are entirely right to get 'het up' about same-sex sexual activity, just as they should get het up about all forms of sexual activity outside heterosexual marriage.

---

[11] Sam Allberry, *Is God Anti-Gay?* (Epsom: The Good Book Company, 2013), p. 28. Emphasis in the original.

6. Does Paul Hate Gays?

The basic claim made in Marcus Greene's paper

In the sixth of the 'Does the Bible Really Say...?' series, Marcus Greene addresses the question, 'Does the Bible Really Say...that St Paul "Hates Gays"?'[1]

At the start of his paper, Greene answers this question by declaring unequivocally: 'St Paul doesn't "hate gays". Short of Jesus, he's our best friend in the whole of the Scriptures.'

In order to justify this claim, he looks first of all at Romans 1:18–32 and I Corinthians 6:9–11, two texts which have been traditionally used to show that Paul disapproved of same-sex sexual activity.

Romans 1:18–32

On Romans 1:18–32, Greene makes two points:

First, that Romans 1:26–27 is not about gay people as such, but only about 'broken' gay people. In Romans 1:28–32, Greene says:

> St Paul is writing about folk who live in brokenness. He's not writing about all relationships, and he's not saying that every person is wicked, evil, greedy, envious, murderous, deceitful, malicious, insolent, inventing evil, faithless, loveless and merciless. He is saying that people (and this means predominantly straight people in our understanding – though Paul wouldn't know the term) who are broken from God are set on this depraved path.[2]

---

[1] Marcus Greene, 'Does the Bible Really Say...that St Paul "Hates Gays"?,' 21 June 2019, at https://viamedia.news/2019/06/21/does-the-bible-really-say-that-st-paul-hates-gays/ (accessed 14 April 2020).
[2] Greene, 'Does the Bible Really Say...that St Paul "Hates Gays"?'.

This in turn means, that:

> even if verses 26 & 27, the middle verses in this passage, are about gay people, in context they are about sinful, broken, idolatrous gay people. They are not a theology helping us to think about how to respond to all LGBT folk in church – any more than verses 28–32 are an understanding of all straight people in church.[1]

Secondly, according to Greene, Paul's argument that same-sex relationships are against nature does not mean such relationships are wrong:

> People get very heated over the words 'natural' and 'unnatural' (better – 'against nature') in Romans 1.26–27. 'There you go – St Paul says being gay is unnatural.'
>
> I was always taught to let the Bible interpret the Bible. And St Paul is a great help in this, because he uses the same words later in Romans.
>
> In Romans 11.24 we again have 'natural' and 'contrary to nature' being used. It's the same language. I know that in Romans 1 some people want to see 'natural' as a pure good and 'against nature' as an unparalleled bad – but in Romans 11, it is we Gentile Christians who are described by St Paul as being grafted into a cultivated olive tree 'against nature', a process which most of us rather depend on, and look at as being a positive thing.
>
> It seems that God can act 'against nature' and in doing so produce something positive. 'Nature' in St Paul is not the final arbiter of good and evil. We do not worship nature – the creation; that's rather the point

---

[1] Greene, 'Does the Bible Really Say...that St Paul "Hates Gays"?'.

of Romans 1! We worship the Creator of nature, who made the creation to be a blessing for us.[2]

1 Corinthians 6:9–11

On 1 Corinthians 6:9–11, Greene rejects the NIV translation of the two Greek words, *malakoi* and *arsenokoitai* in verse 9 as 'men who have sex with men'. He writes:

> Malakoi is well translated by the Authorised Version as 'effeminate', but I think we hear the wrong connotation with that. In Roman culture ... an effeminate man could be one who was seeking the attention of women. Quite the reverse of our expectation. Also, the list of words doesn't link 'arsenokoitai' with 'malakoi' – our presumptions do. If malakoi is a 'ladies man' it fits well with 'adulterers', the word before it. The effect would be – 'the sexually immoral, idolaters, adulterers, men who prey on women, men who prey on men, those who steal, those who are greedy...'

> This is what some of the believers in Corinth were. Not gay – as indeed they aren't being critiqued for being straight – but people displaying the evidences of broken relationship with God. People not loving their neighbour. People draining life from others in order to serve themselves. People who are abusing life to excess because they have not discovered Jesus' gift of living life to the full. That's what they were.[3]

He then further contends that the emphasis of 1 Corinthians 5–7 as a whole is about the sins of straight people:

> 1 Corinthians 5 talks of problems in the fellowship to do with failures in heterosexual marriage. 1

[2] Greene, 'Does the Bible Really Say...that St Paul "Hates Gays"?'.
[3] Greene, 'Does the Bible Really Say...that St Paul "Hates Gays"?'.

Corinthians 7 talks of the gift of marriage in the community – and the gift of celibacy for some in that community. 1 Corinthians 6 is not a bracketed text in the middle with a theology for gay people. It's part of this sweep, and its clear emphasis is on the sins of straight people.

The bigger picture

In the final section of his paper, Greene appeals to Galatians 6:15: 'Neither circumcision nor uncircumcision means anything; what counts is the new creation' and Ephesians 2:15, 19, 'His purpose was to create in himself one new humanity out of the two [Jew and Gentile] thus making peace ... Consequently, you are no longer foreigners and strangers'. These verses, he suggests, give us the bigger picture, the broader Pauline vision, within which we should address questions concerning sexuality.

Paul, he writes:

> had a huge, transformative and truly revolutionary vision of a new community – a new humanity – that broke every social and economic rule in the book. No slave or free, no male or female, no Jew or Gentile. Every believer becoming one in Christ. God's chosen people, holy and dearly loved. Children together by grace through faith.[4]

Greene acknowledges that Paul 'has a huge focus on sexual propriety'.[5] However:

> for some today to think they have a hold on this which begins by making others less free, less human, less reflective of the relational love within the Godhead is

---

[4] Greene, 'Does the Bible Really Say...that St Paul "Hates Gays"?'.
[5] Greene, 'Does the Bible Really Say...that St Paul "Hates Gays"?'.

again to miss the transforming gift of God's new humanity.

Christianity ought never be mistaken for a heterosexual fertility cult – and St Paul's call for abstinence is not aimed at gay folk but perhaps at some of the straight folk who get that emphasis wrong![6]

The problems with Greene's argument

Greene's argument is unconvincing for a number of reasons.

The language of gay and straight

First, Greene's repeated use of the terms 'gay' and 'straight' is misleading. These terms reflect a late twentieth century worldview which classifies people according to their sexual desires. This is not how Paul's anthropology works. For him, as for the Bible as whole, people are not defined by their sexual desires, but by their sex. The categories he works with are not 'gay' or 'straight', but 'male' and female'. In consequence, Paul's sexual ethics are not based on how people should behave as 'gay' or 'straight,' but on how they should behave as those whom God has created as male or female.

Romans 1:26–27

Secondly, Greene misunderstands Paul's argument in Romans 1. What Paul says about same-sex sexual activity in Romans 1:26–27 is not aimed at a particular sub-set of 'gay' people who manifest a broken relationship with God in a way that other 'gay' people do not.

As has already been noted, the very concept of 'gay' people is foreign to Paul's thinking and thus needs to be set aside. Paul's argument is that *all* human beings are broken (see Romans 3:22–23), but that for some men and women this brokenness

---

[6] Greene, 'Does the Bible Really Say...that St Paul "Hates Gays"?'.

manifests itself in having sexual intercourse with members of their own sex.

As Tom Wright notes, the starting point for Paul's argument is that God created men and women to complement each other, to have sexual relations with each other and to be procreative ('fruitful', Genesis 1:28) as a result. In this context, the point that Paul is making about same-sex sexual activity:

> is not simply that 'we Jews don't approve of this,' or 'relationships like this are always unequal or exploitative.' His point is 'this is not what males and females were made for.' Nor is he suggesting that everyone who feels sexually attracted to members of their own sex, or everyone who engages in actual same-sex relations, has got to that point through committing specific acts of idolatry. Nor, again, does he suppose that all those who find themselves in that situation have arrived there by a specific choice to give up heterosexual possibilities. Reading the text like that reflects a modern individualism rather than Paul's larger, all-embracing perspectives. Rather, he is talking about the human race as a whole. His point is not that 'there are some exceptionally wicked people out there who do these revolting things,' but 'the fact that such clear distortions of creator's male-plus-female intention occur in the world indicates that the human race as a whole is guilty of a character twisting idolatry.' He sees the practice of same-sex relations as a sign that the human world in general is out of joint.[7]

Greene's appeal to Romans 11:24 to attempt to give a positive spin to Paul's description of same-sex sexual activity as 'unnatural' (*para phusin*) fails because it does not recognise that in the two different contexts Paul is using the same phrase in two different ways. In Romans 11:24, he is referring to an act of divine grace that goes beyond what is naturally the case,

---

[7] Wright, *Paul For Everyone: Romans Part I*, pp. 22–23.

whereas in Romans 1:26–27 Paul is referring to acts of human sin that go against nature in the sense of being contrary to the good purposes of the creator God.

1 Corinthians 6:9–11

Thirdly, Greene also misunderstands what Paul says in 1 Corinthians 6.

The first point here is that 1 Corinthians 5–7 does not have an 'emphasis on the sins of straight people' for the simple reason that, as we have already noted, the concept of 'straight' people as opposed to 'gay' people does not figure in Paul's theology.[8]

The second point is that Greene has simply chosen to ignore what is now the established scholarly consensus about the meaning of the Greek terms *malakoi* and *arsenokoitai* in 1 Corinthians 6:9. To quote Tom Wright again, these are:

> two words which have been much debated, but which experts have now established, clearly refer to the practice of male homosexuality. The two terms refer respectively to the passive or submissive partner and the active or aggressive one, and Paul places both roles on his list of unacceptable behaviour.[9]

The scholarly consensus about the matter is supported even by 'gay affirming' scholars and the reasons why this is the case are helpfully explained by the distinguished American church historian Eugene Rice (himself supportive of same-sex relationships) in his article on Paul for the online GLBTQ Encyclopedia:

> At 1 Cor. 6:9–10, Paul lists a heterogeneous group of sinners whom he bars from the kingdom of God. The sexual offenders consist of fornicators, adulterers, and

---

[8] Greene, 'Does the Bible Really Say...that St Paul "Hates Gays"?'.

[9] Tom Wright, *Paul for Everyone: 1 Corinthians* (London: SPCK, 2003), p. 69.

two kinds of men: malakoi and arsenokoitai – the nouns are plural and masculine.

The meanings of these Greek nouns have been the subject of lively debate, largely provoked by gay authors anxious to show that Paul and the early church had not intended to condemn homosexuality per se as harshly as has been traditionally supposed, but only a degraded type of pederasty associated with prostitution and child abuse.

Recent scholarship has shown conclusively that the traditional meanings assigned to these words stand. So do the traditional translations: the Latin translation 'commonly used in the church,' and therefore known as the Vulgate, and the English King James Version (KJV).

Malakoi

Malakoi (Latin Vulgate: molles) should have caused no problem. There is ample evidence that in sexual contexts, in both classical and post-classical times, malakos designated the receptive partner in a male same-sex act, a meaning decisively reconfirmed in late antiquity by the physician Caelius Aurelianus when he tells us that the Greeks call malakoi males whom the Latins call molles or subacti, males, that is, who play the receptive role in anal intercourse.

Paul's malakoi, we can say with certainty, are males – boys, youths, or adults – who have consented, either for money or for pleasure, for some perceived advantage or as an act of affectionate generosity, to be penetrated by men.

Arsenokoitai

The word is a verbal noun, and its earliest attestation is in this verse of Paul's. It is a compound of arsen = 'male' and koités = 'a man who lies with (or beds).' And so we have, describing Oedipus, metrokoités, 'a man who lies with his mother,' doulokoités, 'a man who lies with maidservants or female slaves,' polykoités, 'a man who lies with many,' and onokoités, 'a man who lies with donkeys,' said of Christians in a graffito from Carthage of about 195.

Arsenokoitai are therefore 'men who lie with males,' and the Vulgate's masculorum concubitores (where masculorum is an objective genitive), renders the Greek exactly to mean 'men who lie with males,' 'men who sleep with males,' 'men who have sex with males.'

The source of arsenokoitai is in the Greek translation of the Hebrew Bible known as the Septuagint (finished around 130 B.C.E. for the use of Greek-speaking Jews). The Septuagint of Leviticus 18:22 reads: Kai meta arsenos ou koiméthés koitén gynaikeian, and of Lev. 20:13, Kai os an koiméthé meta arsenos koitén gynaikos...; Englished we have, 'With a male you shall not lie the bed/intercourse (koité) of a woman,' and 'Whoever lies with a male the koité of a woman, [both have done an abominable thing, they shall be put to death.]'

The dependence of Paul's arsenokoitai on the Levitical arsenos koitén demonstrates unequivocally its source and confirms his intended meaning. The word was almost certainly coined by Greek-speaking Jews. Understood in the context of what we know about role playing in most ancient same-sex relationships, malakoi are the receptive parties and arsenokoitai the inserters in male-male anal intercourse.[10]

In the light of this evidence, Greene's argument simply collapses. 1 Corinthians 6:9 is about men who have sex with men and Paul says such activity bars people from God's kingdom. However, Paul goes on to say in verse 11 that that is not the end of the matter. How people have behaved in the past is not the last word. To quote Wright once more, Paul's message is that:

> God himself has provided the way in which people can leave their past, and indeed their present, behind, and move towards his future. You can be washed clean, whatever has happened in the past. You can be one of God's special people, whatever you are in the present.[11]

The bigger picture

Fourthly, Greene is absolutely correct when he says that Paul has a 'huge, transformative and truly revolutionary vision of a new community.'[12] Where Greene goes wrong is in failing to recognise that Paul's 'focus on sexual propriety' is an integral part of this vision.

Paul has a vision of a community in which, because of the redeeming work of Christ and through the power of the Holy Spirit, anyone, no matter who they are, or what they have done, can begin to live as the people God made them to be. However, for Paul living in this way involves a call to 'glorify God in your body' (1 Corinthians 6:20) and this means living a life marked either by singleness and sexual abstinence, or sexual faithfulness within (heterosexual) marriage (1 Corinthians

---

[10] Eugene Rice, 'Paul, St.', *GLBTQ Encyclopedia*, 2015, http://www.glbtqarchive.com/ssh/paul_S.pdf (accessed 14 April 2020).

[11] Wright, *Paul For Everyone: 1 Corinthians*, p. 70.

[12] Greene, 'Does the Bible Really Say...that St Paul "Hates Gays"?'.

6:12–7:40). Any other form of sexual activity (including same-sex activity) is *porneia* (sexual immorality), which is something Paul warns all Christians to eschew (see Galatians 5:19, Ephesians 5:3, Colossians 3:5).

This is not, as Greene seems to think, just a message for 'straight' people, but for everybody, whatever their sexual desires. Nor does it mean condemning people to be 'less free, less human, less reflective of the relational love within the Godhead.'[13] There is abundant evidence that people who are same-sex attracted, but who live in accordance with the pattern set out by the apostle Paul can and do live lives that are fully free, fully human and fully reflective of the Triune love of God.[14]

Conclusion

For the reasons explained above, asking whether Paul hates gay people involves asking the wrong question. 'Gay' and 'straight' are simply not categories of his thought.[15] However, what one can properly ask is whether his letters show that Paul hated people who engaged in same-sex sexual activity.

The answer is 'no'. We know he thought such activity was unequivocally sinful, but there is no evidence at all that he hated the people concerned. On the contrary, his letters show that his deepest desire was that they, along with all other people, should flourish as God intended, both in this life and the next. His warnings against sexual immorality were intended to help people achieve this goal and thus were motivated not by hate, but by love.

---

[13] Greene, 'Does the Bible Really Say...that St Paul "Hates Gays"?'.
[14] For the evidence for this point see the material available on and through the 'Living Out' website at https://www.livingout.org/ or the website of the 'True Freedom Trust' at https://truefreedomtrust.co.uk/ (both accessed 13 April 2020).
[15] It is rather like asking if George Washington was a Democrat or a Republican.

7. Why Families Need Fathers and Mothers

In the seventh of the 'Does the Bible Really Say...?' series, Dr Hayley Matthews addresses the question, 'Does the Bible Really Say...that a Family Needs "a Mummy and a Daddy"?'[1]

Dr Matthew's argument

Dr Matthew's answer to this question is 'no' and she gives six reasons for this answer.

First, she argues that in the Bible there is no mention of the 'nuclear family' consisting of a father and mother and their children. Instead, people live in multi-generational households consisting of people related by blood and marriage in a variety of different ways plus servant and slaves.

Secondly, in the Old Testament, we see 'God flouting conventional family ties in unexpected ways through his grace' by choosing to give blessing to people who are not the first-born sons (as in the case of Isaac, Jacob, Judah, Joseph and David) and by passing on his blessing through 'non blood-line outcasts' (such as Ruth, Rahab and Mary).[2]

Thirdly, in the New Testament, Jesus' words in Matthew 12:50 about his true brothers and sisters being those who do the will of his heavenly Father refer not to the creation of a new biological family, but to the formation of a new household in which those who have previously been outcasts are all welcomed as equals and can call God '*Abba*, Father' (Romans 8:15).

---

[1] Hayley Matthews, 'Does the Bible Really Say...that a Family Needs a "Mummy and a Daddy"?', 29 June 2019, at https://viamedia.news/2019/06/29/does-the-bible-really-say-that-families-need-a-mummy-and-a-daddy/ (accessed 14 April 2020).
[2] Matthews, 'Does the Bible Really Say...that a Family Needs a "Mummy and a Daddy"?'.

Fourthly, there are three key turning points in the history of Israel which rely entirely 'upon non-biological family structures', namely the adoption of Moses by Pharaoh's daughter, the adoption of Esther by Mordecai, and the gestation of Jesus 'to an unmarried Mum from Nowheres-ville'.[1]

Fifthly, 'There is biblical precedent for ... households to take many forms; single parents, adoption, surrogacy, foster-care, blended and wide-ranging extended families, male, female or a mixture of the two.'[2]

Sixthly, the gender of parents does not matter because there are numerous reasons why two parents of different genders may not be on the scene and because child psychology tells us 'that what children need are orientation, order, exploration, communication, movement, manipulation of objects, repetition, precision, imagination, facing and constructively responding to error' and 'None of these things are gender specific.'[3]

Dr Matthews's overall conclusion is that:

> Our call, into our own and God's households are far beyond all-too-brief biological couplings but based instead upon grace, forgiveness, fidelity, steadfastness, gentleness, kindness, self-control, selflessness, a sense of the ridiculous if not of humour and love beyond measure in an ever-growing ripple of relationships that ever broadens into the eternal

---

[1] Matthews, 'Does the Bible Really Say...that a Family Needs a "Mummy and a Daddy"?'.

[2] Matthews, 'Does the Bible Really Say...that a Family Needs a "Mummy and a Daddy"?'.

[3] Matthews, 'Does the Bible Really Say...that a Family Needs a "Mummy and a Daddy"?'.

household from which and to which we are called. That's what makes a family.[4]

The problems with this argument

There are a number of problems with this argument.

First, while it is true that in the Bible people tend to live in extended households this does not negate the existence or importance of nuclear families made up of parents and their children.

The first and foundational family unit in the Bible is a nuclear family consisting of Adam and Eve and their children (Genesis 2:18–5:5) and, thereafter, the Bible consistently recognises the existence and importance of the familial relationship between fathers and mothers and their sons and daughters. We can see this, for example, in the command to 'Honour your father and your mother' in Exodus 20:12, in the exhortation in Proverbs 6:20 'My son, keep your father's commandment, and forsake not your mother's teaching' and in the instructions given to husbands and wives and their children in the letters of Paul (Ephesians 5:21–6:4, Colossians 3:18–21, Titus 2:4).

Rather than the household being an alternative to the nuclear family, in the Bible the household is the larger domestic and economic unit within which nuclear families still have a distinct and important existence of their own.

Secondly, while it is perfectly true that God can and does bypass firstborn sons in favour of some other child of the family, none of the examples given by Dr Matthews negate the importance normally given to primogeniture in the Bible, nor do they undercut the importance that the Bible attaches to the biological relationship between parents and children.

If we take the case of Jacob, for instance, we find that Esau, as the firstborn son of Isaac and Rebekah, would have been the

---

[4] Matthews, 'Does the Bible Really Say...that a Family Needs a "Mummy and a Daddy"?'

one to receive a blessing from Isaac had he not 'despised his birthright' and traded it to his brother Jacob for a 'pottage of lentils' (Genesis 25:27–34). For another example, David is chosen to be King of Israel rather than his older brothers because this was a new appointment that was not dependent on family ties and because God, who 'looks on the heart', saw that David rather than his brothers had the qualities needed in a king (1 Samuel 16:1–13). David's place in his family was irrelevant to the issue.

Thirdly, Dr Matthew's depiction of Ruth, Rahab and Mary as 'non-blood line outcasts' is misleading. Ruth and Rahab are not Israelites, but become part of the people of Israel through their commitment to the God of Israel (Ruth 1:16, Josh 2:8–14, 6:25) and both become carriers of God's blessing because they have children as a result of marriage (Ruth 4:13–22, Matthew 1:5). At the point when the angel comes to Mary and she conceives Jesus, Mary is a respectable young Jewish girl and even though she is asked to put her reputation and life in jeopardy by giving birth as a result of a supernatural conception, God ensures that she has a husband and Jesus has an earthly father (Matthew 1:18–25). As numerous nativity scenes testify, Jesus' earthly family ('the holy family') was thus a nuclear family consisting of a mother, a father and a child (with other children being added later).

Fourthly, it is simply not the case that in the New Testament God creates a new household rather than a new family. In the New Testament, the church is indeed the 'household' of God (Ephesians 2:19), but the form this household takes is a new family in which Christians really are brothers and sisters to each other by reason of their relationship to the same heavenly Father. The difference between this family and normal biological families is that this new family is a result of the supernatural action of God rather than human sexual activity. This point is made explicitly in John 1:12–13 (RSV):

> But to all who received him, who believed in his name, he gave power to become children of God; who were

born, not of blood nor of the will of the flesh nor of the
will of man, but of God.

Fifthly, it is true that both Moses and Esther were adopted and
that Mary was not married to Joseph when Jesus was
conceived. In these three cases, God does indeed work through
'non-biological family structures'. However, the fact that he
does so for specific reasons on these occasions does not negate
the importance of biological family structures as the normal
means which God has established to take forward his purposes
in creation.

In Genesis, God creates human beings in his image and
likeness as male and female and commands than to 'be fruitful
and multiply' (Genesis 1:26–28). He then establishes marriage
between one man and one woman as the family structure
through which this command is to be fulfilled (Genesis 2:18–
25) and this ordinance remains in place throughout the rest of
the Bible.

Sixthly, this means that while it is true that we see lots of
different types of households and families in the Bible, when
children are not the offspring of a marital relationship between
a husband and wife, or when a mother or father is not on the
scene, this always means that something has gone wrong.
There is no case in the Bible in which an alternative family
structure to a father and a mother and their children is seen as
equally desirable. When children are born out of wedlock, or
there is a polygamous family structure, or one or both parents
are dead and there are thus widows and orphans, this is a sign
of the brokenness of the world stemming from the Fall and not
what would have been the case had God's original intentions
for his human creatures been fulfilled.

It is true, as the charity Home for Good argues, that adoption
and fostering are extremely important forms of Christian
service that can achieve an enormous amount of good.[5]

---

[5] Home for Good at https://www.homeforgood.org.uk/ (accessed 18
April 2020).

However, the good that they achieve lies in helping to mend that which has been broken. Were this not a broken world, neither adoption nor fostering would be required since all children would be living with their married parents.

Seventhly, Dr Matthews' reference to the findings of child psychology fails to acknowledge that decades of research evidence clearly shows that both the marital status and the sex of a child's parents does matter. As David Ribar puts it:

> Reams of social science and medical research convincingly show that children who are raised by their married, biological parents enjoy better physical, cognitive, and emotional outcomes, on average, than children who are raised in other circumstances.[6]

In similar fashion, Michael Nazir-Ali notes:

> the mounting evidence that children who grow up with both their parents are, on the whole, better off than children with lone parents or step-parents, whether that is in terms of mental health, educational performance, crime or sexual behaviour. This is not, in any way, to devalue the sometimes heroic effects of loving single parents or step-parents. It is simply to note the importance of biologically-related families against the frantic and increasingly successful efforts to deconstruct them.[7]

What all this evidence indicates is that pattern of family life ordained by God – in which children are brought up by their married biological parents – is the gold standard for child well-

---

[6] David Ribar, 'Why marriage matters for child wellbeing' in *The Future of Children: Marriage and Child Wellbeing Revisited,* Vol. 25, No. 2, 2015, p. 12.
[7] Michael Nazir-Ali, *Faith, Freedom and the Future* (London: Wilberforce Publications, 2016), p. 126.

being and needs to be supported accordingly by both the church and the state.[8]

Finally, it is not the case, as Dr Matthews suggests, that 'what makes a family' are the characteristics of 'grace, forgiveness, fidelity, steadfastness, gentleness, kindness, self-control, selflessness, a sense of the ridiculous if not of humour, and love.' For a family to function properly, these elements will certainly need to be present, but they are not what makes a family. A human family is created through biology, marriage or adoption, while God's eternal family is created through supernatural grace received through faith and baptism.

Conclusion

Dr Matthews has not succeeded in showing that the Bible does not say that 'a family needs a Mummy and a Daddy'. On the contrary, the Bible tells us that the form of family life ordained by God at creation is one which requires a father and mother. God ordained that human beings should be fruitful and multiply and that this should happen through two people of the opposite sex entering into marriage and having children as a result. Furthermore, while the effects of the Fall mean that this pattern of family life will never be perfect, the evidence we have shown that it is the pattern that is most conducive to human flourishing.

What we can say, therefore, is that the testimony of both Scripture and natural reason show us that human beings need families and these families need fathers and mothers.

---

[8] For a detailed study setting out the evidence for this claim see Brenda Almond, *The Fragmenting Family* (Oxford: Clarendon Press, 2006).

8. Why Grace does not Destroy Nature

Professor Percy's five-fold argument

In the eighth of the 'Does the Bible Really Say...?' series, Professor Martyn Percy addresses the topic, 'Does the Bible Really...Advocate the "Nuclear Family"?'[1]

In his article, Professor Percy gives five reasons for rejecting the idea that Christianity is 'right behind the nuclear family'.[2]

First, he appeals to the teaching of Jesus, declaring:

> Jesus advocated leaving one's parents for the sake of the Kingdom. The siblings too, got some short shrift from Jesus. He told his disciples to go do likewise, more or less. Moreover, don't even think about loitering at your parents' funerals; there is kingdom work to be done. The dead can bury the dead.[3]

Secondly, he argues that the Bible 'contains many patterns of family life' and that the Old Testament in particular 'offers us dozens – literally – of 'family patterns', which 'should not necessarily be honoured today.'[4] As an example, he refers to the story of Rachel and Leah in Genesis 29–30, both of whom are married to Jacob, and both of whom offer him their maids so that he can beget children by them.

Thirdly, he argues that the founders of four of the world's great religions, Moses, the Buddha, Mohammed and Jesus were all adopted:

---

[1] Martyn Percy, 'Does the Bible Really...Advocate the "Nuclear Family"?', 5 July 2019, at https://viamedia.news/2019/07/05/does-the-bible-really-advocate-the-nuclear-family/ (accessed 14 April 2020).
[2] Percy, 'Does the Bible Really...Advocate the "Nuclear Family"?'.
[3] Percy, 'Does the Bible Really...Advocate the "Nuclear Family"?'.
[4] Percy, 'Does the Bible Really...Advocate the "Nuclear Family"?'.

Moses was abandoned by his birth mother and left to float in a small coracle in the River Nile, and had the good fortune to be picked up by the daughter of one of the Pharaohs, and nurtured as one of her own. Mohammed was orphaned at the age of six, or perhaps earlier, and was brought up by his uncle in the ancient city of Makka. The Buddha's mother died when he was less than a week old, and he was raised by her sister. Jesus, of course, according to Christian orthodoxy is not exactly the child of Joseph, since Christian tradition claims no human intervention in his genesis. Although Mary is clearly his mother, Joseph is not his biological father.[1]

According to Professor Percy this matters because it places the dynamic of adoption at the heart of these religious traditions.

Fourthly, the early church based itself not on the pattern of the nuclear family, but on the pattern of an *oikos*, an 'extended household incorporating kith and kin, servants, slaves, tutors, workers, dependents and contributors.'[2]

Fifthly, as an *oikos* the church was an outward facing body that 'took to adoption quite naturally' and adoption is something that is central to the church's life:

just as churches, congregations and individuals Christians understand or experience themselves as, in some sense, 'adopted' by God (as Paul suggests), so they in turn, find themselves adopting others.[3]

It is for this reason, Professor Percy contends, that:

the churches, at their best, function like adoption and foster homes. They welcome the unwelcome; they love the unloved; they embrace the excluded. The Church

---

[1] Percy, 'Does the Bible Really...Advocate the "Nuclear Family"?'.
[2] Percy, 'Does the Bible Really...Advocate the "Nuclear Family"?'.
[3] Percy, 'Does the Bible Really...Advocate the "Nuclear Family"?'.

was not meant to be a cult or a club for members, any more than the Christian vision for 'family' was ever meant to be 'nuclear'. It wasn't.

The early church took in widows and orphans. The early church was extensive and open in character. It embraced slave and free, Jew and Gentile. It will have embraced married and unmarried, and young and old, citizen and alien. If the Church wants to recover a vision for mission and evangelism, and plead for the restoration of moral foundations in contemporary society, then appealing to the sanctity of the 'nuclear family' is not the way forward.[4]

How should we respond to this argument?

The first thing to note is that Professor Percy seems to be operating with a very misleading understanding of what is meant by a 'nuclear family'.

Implicit in his overall approach to the significance of the nuclear family is a contrast between a nuclear family and a body that is open to adopting the outsider. His central argument seems to be that the church should be the latter rather than the former.

However, the generally accepted definition of a nuclear family is 'the basic family unit consisting of the mother and father with their children.'[5] What is important to note is that these children are not necessarily the biological children of the parents concerned. From time immemorial, children have become permanent members of nuclear families through adoption, with the mother and father becoming their mother and father and the other children in the family becoming their brothers and sisters. Furthermore, nuclear families have often

---

4 Percy, 'Does the Bible Really...Advocate the "Nuclear Family"?'.
5 'Nuclear family', *The Chambers Dictionary*, 9th ed. (Edinburgh: Chambers Harrap, 2003), p. 1023.

had other people living with them as 'part of the family' for greater or lesser periods of time, whether other family members, foster children, or just people in need of a home.

Professor Percy's suggestion that nuclear families are inherently closed entities which exclude outsiders is thus simply untrue.

Secondly, he is also misleading in his account of the teaching of Jesus. Although he does not give specific references, he seems to be referring to two passages from Luke's Gospel.

The first of these references is in Luke 14:

> If anyone comes to me and does not hate his own father and mother and wife and children and brothers and sisters, yes, and even his own life, he cannot be my disciple (Luke 14:26).

At first sight, this appears to be a clear repudiation by Jesus of all family ties. However, this would contradict Jesus' own criticism in Mark 7:9–13 of those who reject their family responsibilities, and, as George Caird notes in his commentary on Luke, this is not actually what Jesus' words mean:

> To hate father and mother did not mean on the lips of Jesus what it conveys to the Western reader ... The semitic mind is comfortable only with extremes – light and darkness, truth and falsehood, love and hate – primary colours with no half-shades of compromise in between. The semitic way of saying 'I prefer this to that' is 'I like this and hate that' (cf. Genesis 29:10–31, Deuteronomy 21:15–17). Thus for the followers of Jesus, to hate their families meant giving the family second place in their affections. Ties of kinship must not be allowed to interfere with their absolute commitment to the kingdom.[6]

---

[6] George Caird, *Saint Luke* (Harmondsworth: Pelican, 1963), pp. 178–179.

The second reference Professor Percy seems to be referring to is in Luke 9 where we read:

> To another he said, 'Follow me.' But he said, 'Lord, let me first go and bury my father.' And Jesus said to him, 'Leave the dead to bury their own dead. But as for you, go and proclaim the kingdom of God.' Yet another said, 'I will follow you, Lord, but let me first say farewell to those at my home.' Jesus said to him, 'No one who puts his hand to the plough and looks back is fit for the kingdom of God (Luke 9:59–62).

This again looks like Jesus rejecting the importance of family duties, but as Caird points out, the point of the saying is rather to warn would-be disciples,

> to reckon with the conflict of loyalties which discipleship inevitably brings. In normal circumstances it is good that a man should have a home of his own in which he can perform his acts of filial piety to his parents, whether in life or in death, and show affection to kindred and friends. All this is part of that family life which God has graciously appointed for his children. But a man must be prepared to sacrifice security, duty, and affection, if he is to respond to the call of the kingdom, a call so urgent and imperative that all other loyalties must give way before it.[7]

What this means is that Jesus does not teach that Christians have to leave their parents or reject their siblings. What he does say is that even family ties – vitally important though they are – must take second place in our loyalties to the demands of God and his kingdom. God has to come even before family if there is ever a conflict between them.

---

[7] Caird, *Saint Luke*, p. 141.

Professor Percy's second point – that there are many patterns of family life in the Bible and these should not necessarily be honoured today – is true so far as it goes. We are indeed not called to follow dysfunctional forms of family life such as we find in Genesis 29–30. However, we know this because the Bible itself tells us that such forms of family life are a departure from what God ordained at creation

To repeat what I said in my response to Dr Hayley Matthews in the previous chapter:

> In Genesis, God creates human beings in his image and likeness as male and female and commands than to 'be fruitful and multiply' (Genesis 1:26–28, RSV). He then establishes marriage between one man and one woman as the family structure through which this command is to be fulfilled (Genesis 2:18–25) and this ordinance remains in place throughout the rest of the Bible.

> ... This means that while it is true that we see lots of different types of households and families in the Bible, when children are not the offspring of a marital relationship between a husband and wife, or when a mother or father is not on the scene, this always means that something has gone wrong. There is no case in the Bible in which an alternative family structure to a father and a mother and their children is seen as equally desirable. When children are born out of wedlock, or there is a polygamous family structure, or one or both parents are dead and there are thus widows and orphans, this is a sign of the brokenness of the world stemming from the Fall and not what would have been the case had God's original intentions for his human creatures been fulfilled.

However, the existence of such broken forms of family life does not negate the importance of the pattern of family life instituted by God at creation. This pattern remains a key part of God's provision for human well-being and so Christians need to live within it themselves and to teach and support others to do the same.

Moving on to Professor Percy's third point, what he says about Moses and Jesus requires important qualification.

First of all, Moses was not 'abandoned by his birth mother.'[8] The story in Exodus 2:1–10 is instead about how Moses' mother and sister ensured that he survived Pharaoh's threat to kill all the sons of the Hebrew people. The story tells us about how a Jewish family took care of one of its own in the face of the threat of genocide and how this action then became the basis for subsequent deliverance of the Jewish people as a whole. It is thus a story precisely about the importance of family ties.

With regard to Jesus, it is not true that Christian orthodoxy says that there was no 'human intervention in the birth of Jesus'.[9] What it says is that there was an indispensable human role in his birth which consisted in Mary providing the egg that was made fertile by God, carrying the resultant baby to term, and giving birth to him when the time came (Luke 1:26–2:7). The traditional title *theotokos* ('mother of God'), used with reference to Mary, expresses this point by insisting that in his human nature God the Son did have a mother and that that mother was Mary.

The biblical accounts of the birth of Jesus are about how Jesus, who already had a familial relationship with God the Father from all eternity as God the Son, also acquired a human family consisting of his human biological mother, Mary and also a human father, Joseph with siblings then coming along later. Rather than having no family, Jesus thus has two.

Turning to Professor Percy's fourth point, as I also observed in the previous chapter, it is mistaken to argue as he does that the early church was a household rather than being a family:

---

[8] Percy, 'Does the Bible Really...Advocate the "Nuclear Family"?'.
[9] Percy, 'Does the Bible Really...Advocate the "Nuclear Family"?'.

it is simply not the case that in the New Testament God creates a new household rather than a new family. In the New Testament, the church is indeed the 'household' of God (Ephesians 2:19), but the form this household takes is a new family in which Christians really are brothers and sisters to each other by reason of their relationship to the same heavenly Father. The difference between this family and normal biological families is that this new family is a result of the supernatural action of God rather than human sexual activity. This point is made explicitly in John 1:12–13 (RSV):

'But to all who received him, who believed in his name, he gave power to become children of God; who were born, not of blood nor of the will of the flesh nor of the will of man, but of God.'

We have already noted that the Bible tells us that Jesus was, and is, a member of two families. He is the eternal Son of God, but also a member of human nuclear family with a mother and a father and brothers and sisters. What the Bible also tells us that all Christians also belong to two families. They are members of their earthly families, but they are also by grace, through adoption (Galatians 4:1–7), members of an eternal heavenly family with God as their Father and Jesus and all other Christians as their brothers and sisters.

Living rightly as Christians means living rightly as a member of both families. As members of human families, Christians are called to love and honour their parents and to love and care for their spouse and their children (Ephesians 5:21–6:4, Colossians 3:18–21, Titus 2:4–5) and as members of the heavenly family they are called also to love God and all their Christian brothers and sisters (1 John 4:7–21).

With regard to Professor Percy's final point, there is no contradiction between the church affirming the sanctity of the nuclear family and being an outward facing body ready to welcome everybody regardless of who they are, or the circumstances of their lives.

God has created human beings to live in families consisting of married parents and their children and so it is the calling of Christians to affirm this truth and the consequent importance of everyone living rightly as members of such families. However, God has also created the new supernatural family of the church and it is the calling of Christians to welcome everyone into this new family and to teach what it means to live rightly as a member of it. That is the point of the Great Commission in Matthew 28:18–20.

Conclusion

For Professor Percy, it seems, grace abolishes nature. For him, all that matters is the existence of the church created by the grace of adoption with natural human families totally disappearing from view. However, as Thomas Aquinas famously affirms '*Gratia non tollit naturam, sed perficit*' (grace does not destroy nature, but perfects it).[10] In the case we are considering, grace perfects nature because it allows those who are members of natural families to become members of the eternal heavenly family without ceasing to be what they already are.

There are, of course, as Jesus warned us, occasions when we may need to put the requirements of our membership of our heavenly family before membership of our human families, but the latter still remains in place and we are called to honour it as much as possible.

In addition, it is also important to note that when human families are Christian families, membership of the earthly and heavenly families should go together, with the human family acting as what the Christian tradition has called the 'domestic church', in which people are brought up from childhood by

---

[10] St Thomas Aquinas, *Summa Theologiae*, I, I, 8 ad 2.

their human parents to know the truth about God and what it means to live as his children.

This is the vision of family life which lies, for example, behind Luther's *Small Catechism* of 1529 which is designed for the father as the head of the family to teach to the household.[11] It is the vision that is also behind the statement in the *Book of Common Prayer* marriage service that marriage was ordained 'for the procreation of children, to be brought up in the fear and nurture of the Lord and to the praise of his holy name.'[12]

---

[11] Martin Luther, *Small Catechism* in Mark Noll (ed.) *Confessions and Catechisms of the Reformation* (Vancouver: Regent College Publishing, 2004), chapter 4.
[12] 'The Form of Solemnization of Matrimony', *Book of Common Prayer*, 1662.

9. Is it Ever Right to Refuse Baptism?

What Bishop David says in his article

In the ninth of the 'Does the Bible Really Say...?' series, Bishop David Gillett considers the question, 'Does the Bible Really Say...that Baptism Should be Withheld from Some People?'[1]

In his article, Bishop David does not directly answer the question contained in the title. What he does instead is to contrast the position of the Church of England with that of the Presbyterian Church of Ireland. The latter, he says, 'refuses baptism to those in a same sex marriage and to their children' whereas, in spite of the approach taken by some members of the clergy, the policy of the Church of England is that those in same-sex sexual relationships and their children should be admitted to baptism and that where there are two parents of the same sex they should both be listed as mothers or fathers in the baptism register.[2]

According to Bishop David, the welcoming approach of the Church of England corresponds to something:

> deep in the DNA of Christian faith that impels us to receive and welcome all who come to us – our first instinct is naturally to want to extend the loving welcome of God in Christ. Of course, in the baptism service itself, the godparents or the adult candidates will go on to make a profession of faith but this follows on from the wholehearted and sincere welcome which

---

[1] David Gillett, Does the Bible Really Say...that Baptism Should be Withheld from Some People?', 12 July 2019, at https://viamedia.news/2019/07/12/does-the-bible-really-say-that-baptism-should-be-withheld-from-some-people/ (accessed 14 April 2020).
[2] Gillett, 'Does the Bible Really Say...that Baptism Should be Withheld from Some People?'.

has first been extended – the kind of welcome that
Jesus demonstrated when the disciples were minded
to be exclusionary in their approach. 'Then little
children were being brought to him in order that he
might lay hands on them and pray. The disciples
spoke sternly to those who brought them; but Jesus
said, "let the little children come to me, and do not
stop them; for it is to such as these that the kingdom
of heaven belongs." (Matthew 19: 13).'[1]

According to Bishop David, this welcoming approach also:

reflects the outcome of the quick thinking which no
doubt Philip had to do when the Ethiopian Eunuch
made his request for baptism – 'Look, here is water!
What is to prevent me from being baptized?' In this
case, as the enquirer was both a eunuch and a Gentile
he did not fulfill the usual requirements to which
Philip was accustomed. Many would have excluded
him from full involvement in the worshiping
community. In Philip's eyes, following Jesus'
example, the Ethiopian's difference was no bar to full
inclusion. (Acts 8.26–40)[2]

The conclusion that Bishop David reaches at the end of his
article is that:

Many of us are frustrated by the Church of England's
ponderously slow and drawn out process of deciding
on full equality for LGBTQ+ people. At times it can
seem to many that there is a deliberate policy of delay
in facilitating progress towards the eventual
acceptance of equal marriage. However, in contrast,
there is a clear acceptance that baptism is fully

---

[1] Gillett, 'Does the Bible Really Say...that Baptism Should be Withheld
from Some People?'..
[2] Gillett, 'Does the Bible Really Say...that Baptism Should be Withheld
from Some People?'.

inclusive. Meanwhile we are in the ironic situation where baptism, the foundation sacrament within the Church, is open to all whereas lawfully married same sex couples are barred from both a church marriage and the possibility of ordination.

The hope and prayers of an increasing number from all traditions within the Church – be they catholic, reformed, liberal or evangelical, formal or informal – are focused on full equality for LGBTQ+ people in all sacraments and ordinances from baptism through the whole of life – for themselves, their partners and their ministries.[3]

How should we respond to what Bishop David says?

The current position of the Church of England

To start off with, we have to acknowledge that what Bishop David says about the approach taken by the Church of England is factually correct. The House of Bishops has made clear in its statements on civil partnerships and same-sex marriage that being in a same-sex sexual relationship should not be a bar to baptism, and that likewise baptism cannot lawfully be refused to children for whom those in same-sex sexual relationships have parental responsibility.[4]

Paragraphs 23–25 of the 2005 document 'Civil Partnerships: A pastoral statement from the House of Bishops of the Church of England' state:

> 23. The House considers that lay people who have registered civil partnerships ought not to be asked to give assurances about the nature of their relationship

---

[3] Gillett, 'Does the Bible Really Say...that Baptism Should be Withheld from Some People?'.

[4] Human biology means that no child has two biological parents of the same sex. What is possible however, is for two people of the same sex to have legal parental responsibility for a child.

before being admitted to baptism, confirmation and communion. Issues in Human Sexuality made it clear that, while the same standards apply to all, the Church did not want to exclude from its fellowship those lay people of gay or lesbian orientation who, in conscience, were unable to accept that a life of sexual abstinence was required of them and instead chose to enter into a faithful, committed relationship.

24. The Adoption Act 2003 allows for couples that are not married, opposite-sex and same-sex, to adopt children. The Civil Partnership Act includes legislation about children and reflects an expectation that some people who register civil partnerships will have children in their care. While the House of Bishops recognises many in the Church have reservations about these developments, we believe an unconditional welcome should be given to children in our churches, regardless of the structure of the family in which they are being brought up.

25. In relation to infant baptism, Canon B22.4 makes it clear that, while baptism can be delayed for the purposes of instruction (including on marriage and the family), it cannot be refused. The responsibility for taking vows on behalf of the infant rests with the parents and godparents. Provided there is a willingness, following a period of instruction to give those vows, priests cannot refuse to baptise simply because those caring for the infant are not, in their view, living in accordance with the Church's teaching.[5]

---

[5] The Church of England, 'Civil Partnerships: A pastoral statement from the House of Bishops of the Church of England', 25 July 2005, https://www.churchofengland.org/sites/default/files/2017-11/House%20of%20Bishops%20Statement%20on%20Civil%20Partnerships%202005.pdf (accessed 18 April 2020).

Paragraphs 15–18 of the Appendix to 'The House of Bishops Pastoral Guidance on Same Sex Marriage' (issued in 2014) draw on the 2005 document and reach the same conclusion. They state:

> 15. In *Issues in Human Sexuality* the House affirmed that, while the same standards of conduct applied to all, the Church of England should not exclude from its fellowship those lay people of gay or lesbian orientation who, in conscience, were unable to accept that a life of sexual abstinence was required of them and who, instead, chose to enter into a faithful, committed sexually active relationship.

> 16. Consistent with that, we said in our 2005 pastoral statement that lay people who had registered civil partnerships ought not to be asked to give assurances about the nature of their relationship before being admitted to baptism, confirmation and holy communion, or being welcomed into the life of the local worshipping community more generally.

> 17. We also noted that the clergy could not lawfully refuse to baptize children on account of the family structure or lifestyle of those caring for them, so long as they and the godparents were willing to make the requisite baptismal promises following a period of instruction.

> 18, We recognise the many reasons why couples wish their relationships to have a formal status. These include the joys of exclusive commitment and also extend to the importance of legal recognition of the relationship. To that end, civil partnership continues to be available for same sex couples. Those same sex couples who choose to marry should be welcomed into the life of the worshipping community and not be subjected to questioning about their lifestyle. Neither

they nor any children they care for should be denied access to the sacraments.[6]

Bishop David is also correct in what he says about the guidance given by the Legal Advisory Commission of the General Synod in 2017 about what should be put in the Baptism register when two people of the same sex have a shared parental responsibility. The guidance says:

> (a) the columns referring to fathers and mothers must be read as relating to those currently holding parental responsibility for the child, who may or may not be a biological parent (or in exceptional circumstances to those entitled to exercise the power under section 2(5) of the Children Act 1989);
>
> (b) where persons of the same sex share parental responsibility their names should both be inserted in the same gender specific column, namely, Father's name or Mother's name.[7]

However, the fact that Bishop David is factually correct about the position of the Church of England does not mean that that position is itself correct theologically. It may be, or it may or not be. It is to this issue we now turn.

---

[6] The Church of England, 'House of Bishops Pastoral Guidance on Same Sex Marriage', 15 February 2014, https://www.churchofengland.org/more/media-centre/news/house-bishops-pastoral-guidance-same-sex-marriage (accessed 18 April 2020).

[7] The Church of England, Legal Advisory Commission of the General Synod, 'Baptism of Children: Parental Responsibility and Same Sex Couples,' 2017, https://www.churchofengland.org/sites/default/files/2017-12/registration%20of%20baptisms%20final.pdf (accessed 18 April 2020).

Assessing the Church of England's position

In assessing the Church of England's position, we need to be clear at the outset that, according to the teaching of Holy Scripture, marriage is a relationship between one man and one woman, the sole legitimate place of sexual intercourse is within marriage, and that all forms of sexual intercourse outside marriage (including between two people of the same-sex) are what the Bible calls *porneia*, illicit sexual activity that renders someone unclean in the sight of God (Mark 7:21–23). The calling of Christians is to 'glorify God in your body' (1 Corinthians 6:20,) and this involves refraining from all forms of *porneia*, including same-sex sexual activity.[8]

However, the question we need to consider in this article is not simply whether same- sex sexual activity is sinful, but whether someone may rightly be baptised if they are in same-sex sexual relationship themselves, or if they are a child for whom two people in a same-sex sexual relationship have parental responsibility.

We cannot resolve this latter issue simply by appealing to Jesus' welcoming children in Matthew 19:13–15 or Philip's baptism of the Ethiopian eunuch in Acts 8:36–38. Both of these passages indicate in general terms the importance of welcoming those who come forward for baptism, whether they are children or adults. However, neither of these passages address the specific issue we are interested in and, in fact, this issue is not specifically addressed anywhere in the Bible.

How, then, can we resolve it? What we have to do is to go back to first principles and look at the nature of baptism.

---

[8] For the evidence to support this point see Brown, *Can You Be Gay and Christian;* Gagnon, *The Bible and Homosexual Practice;* and Ian Paul, *Same-sex Unions: The key biblical texts* (Cambridge: Grove Books, 2014).

A good place to begin is the definition of baptism contained in the Catechism in the *Book of Common Prayer*. This runs as follows:

> **Question:** What is the outward visible sign or form in Baptism?
> **Answer:** Water: wherein the person is baptized, In the Name of the Father, and of the Son, and of the Holy Ghost.
>
> **Question:** What is the inward and spiritual grace?
> **Answer:** A death unto sin, and a new birth unto righteousness: for being by nature born in sin, and the children of wrath, we are hereby made the children of grace.
>
> **Question:** What is required of persons to be baptized?
> **Answer:** Repentance, whereby they forsake sin: and faith, whereby they steadfastly believe the promises of God, made to them in that Sacrament.[9]

If we unpack this definition, we find that at baptism a gift is given by God, the gift of death to sin and a new birth unto righteousness (John 3:1–8, Romans 6:1–11).

In order for this gift to be given and received two things have to happen: (a) There needs to be baptism with water in the name of the Father, the Son and the Holy Spirit (Matthew 28:19) and (b) the person baptised needs to repent and believe (Acts 2:38, Mark 16:16). This repentance and faith is expressed formally through the promises made in the baptismal liturgy, but it is something that then needs to be lived out in the whole of someone's life then and thereafter.

This understanding of baptism raises the obvious question of why it is right to baptise infants who are necessarily incapable

---

[9] A Catechism, *Book of Common Prayer*, 1662.

of repentance and faith. This question is answered in the Catechism as follows:

> **Question:** Why then are infants baptized, when by reason of their tender age they cannot perform them?
> **Answer:** Because they promise them both by their sureties: which promise, when they come to age, themselves are bound to perform.[10]

What this is saying is that when an infant is baptised those speaking on their behalf (their 'sureties' – today parents and godparents) make promises for them and the child then accepts and performs these promises when they are old enough to do so. In the language of the *Book of Common Prayer* confirmation service they thus 'ratify and confirm' the promises of repentance and faith made on their behalf.

What we now have to decide is how this understanding of baptism relates to the question of whether those who are in a same-sex sexual relationship, or children for whom those in a same-sex sexual relationship have parental responsibility, can properly be baptised.

Why the House of Bishops' statements are unhelpful

To start off with, we have to note that the reference made in both of the House of Bishops statements to what is said in *Issues in Human Sexuality* is unhelpful. These statements refer to paragraph 5.6 of *Issues,* which discusses lay people in same-sex relationships. This paragraph states:

> At the same time there are others who are conscientiously convinced that this way of abstinence is not the best for them, and that they have more hope of growing in love for God and neighbour with the help of a loving and faithful homophile[11] partnership, in intention lifelong, where mutual self-giving

---

[10] Catechism, *BCP.*
[11] 'Homophile' here means 'homosexual'.

includes the physical expression of their attachment. In responding to this conviction it is important to bear in mind the historic tension in Christian ethical thinking between the God given moral order and the freedom of the moral agent. While insisting that conscience needs to be informed in the light of that order, Christian tradition also contains an emphasis on respect for free conscientious judgment where the individual has seriously weighed the issues involved. The homophile is only one in a range of such cases. While unable, therefore, to commend the way of life just described as in itself as faithful a reflection of God's purposes in creation as the heterophile,[12] we do not reject those who sincerely believe it is God's call to them. We stand alongside them in the fellowship of the church, all alike dependent upon the undeserved grace of God.[13]

The problem with this paragraph is that it suggests that committed same-sex sexual relationships between lay people are acceptable in the church because the people concerned sincerely believe in all good conscience that this is what is right for them. What the paragraph is saying, in effect, is that sincerity is enough to render a form of sexual behaviour acceptable within the life of the church.

However, as Paul notes in 1 Corinthians 5:8, commenting precisely on the issue of sexual behaviour in response to a member of the church in Corinth being in an illicit sexual relationship with his father's wife (1 Corinthians 5:1) , the life of Christians has to be marked not by sincerity alone, but by 'sincerity and truth.' Christians not only need to be sincere in their behaviour (in the sense of acting in accordance with their convictions), but how they behave needs to be based on truth, the truth of how God created human beings to be. To put it

---

[12] 'Heterophile' here means 'heterosexual'.
[13] The House of Bishops, *Issues in Human Sexuality* (London: Church House Publishing, 1991), p. 41.

another way, Christian behaviour needs to be marked by a sincere commitment to the objective truth of how people ought to behave.

The paragraph from *Issues* detaches sincerity from truth and for this reason it is misleading. People may indeed sincerely believe that what God wills for them is that they should be in a same-sex sexual relationship, but this belief is contrary to the truth and does not render their behaviour any less sinful.[14]

We cannot say, therefore, that we can baptise people because their same-sex sexual behaviour really doesn't matter since they believe that it is OK. We have to acknowledge that, whatever they think about the issue, their behaviour is sinful and that this sin matters.

What we also cannot say is that it is right to baptise the children of same-sex couples because Canon B 22:4 gives no option in the matter. The bishops are right about what the Canon says. It is clear that the baptism of children may be delayed for instruction, but cannot be refused. However, this does not mean that the Canon is right.

So how should we assess whether it is right to baptise those in same- sex sexual relationships or the children for whom they are responsible? Should the nature of their relationship be viewed as in itself an absolute impediment to baptism?

---

[14] It is interesting to note that the subsequent paragraphs of *Issues in Human Sexuality* (5.7–5.10) the question of respect for conscientious conviction disappears in relation to bisexuality, promiscuous same-sex relationships and paedophilia. These are seen as wrong in all circumstances with nothing being said about the possible conscientious convictions of the people involved. What *Issues* never explains is why conscience should be respected in relation to some forms of behaviour and not others.

Should a same-sex sexual relationship be seen as an absolute impediment to baptism?

Two different approaches to this issue are taken by those who accept the biblical teaching that same-sex sexual relationships are sinful.

Approach A

The first approach holds that the existence of a same-sex sexual relationship is an absolute impediment. This approach begins from the Anglican conviction, derived from the Bible, that baptism needs to involve repentance and faith. As we have already noted, this means that those who come to baptism need to not only 'steadfastly believe the promises of God, made to them in that Sacrament' but also 'forsake sin' since that is what repentance involves.[15]

Those who are in a same-sex sexual relationship have not forsaken sin since they are still involved in it. Hence, when they say in the baptism service that they repent 'of the sins that separate us from God and neighbour', they are not telling the truth.[16] Their relationship show that they have not yet truly repented.

What follows from this is that someone in a same-sex sexual relationship may indeed receive the 'outward visible sign' of baptism – but their lack of repentance means that they will not receive the 'inward spiritual grace'. Furthermore, not only will they not receive the spiritual benefits promised to those who receive baptism rightly, but the perjury involved in saying that they repent when they do not will actually make their situation before God worse. Rather than their sin being taken away, it will have been added to.

In addition, if a church allows someone to say that they repent of their sin while they are in same-sex sexual relationship, this

---

[15] Catechism, *BCP.*
[16] The Decision in Holy Baptism, *Common Worship*, 2006.

must mean that either the church holds that their relationship is not really sinful, or that this sin does not need to be repented of – neither of which are positions that a church should take. If a church says, as it should, that same-sex sexual relationships are sinful, then this means that a church must not baptise someone who is still in such a relationship.

With regard to the children for whom those in same-sex relationships have parental responsibility, the argument put forward by those who take this approach is that children share in the same covenant relationship with God as their parents. In the words of Archbishop Cranmer, 'they are participants in the same divine promise and covenant.'[17]

For those children whose parents are in a right relationship with God through repentance and faith, this shared covenant relationship brings spiritual blessing. However, those in same-sex sexual relationships are not in a right relationship with God, due to lack of repentance. It follows that baptising children for whom they are responsible would not only not make those children's spiritual condition better, but would actually make it worse, since they would then be implicated in the false promise of repentance made on their behalf.

Furthermore, since those living in same-sex sexual relationships will bring up children to believe that such relationships are not sinful, these children's alienation from God will be increased as they grow older and come to accept this belief for themselves. If a church does not address the issue of the sinfulness of same-sex relationships by saying 'no' to a request for baptism, it will be conniving with this downward trajectory.

The last point that needs to be noted, is that those who take this approach would never simply tell those in same-sex relationships to go away. They would do their best to welcome

---

[17] Thomas Cranmer, *Reformatio Legum Ecclesiasticarum* 2:18 in Gerald Bray (ed.), *Tudor Church Reform* (Woodbridge: Boydell Press/Church of England Record Society, 2005). p. 201.

them and their children and they would use the period of instruction allowed under Canon B22.4 to work with them to help them reach a position where they were no longer in a same-sex sexual relationship and so the impediment to baptism would no longer exist.

Approach B

The second approach holds that the existence of a same sex-sexual relationship is not an absolute impediment to baptism.

To take the issue of the baptism of adults first, those who take this second approach would agree that same-sex sexual relationships are sinful and that those in such relationships should be encouraged to cease being in them. However, they would say that there are number of reasons why this fact should not prevent people who are still in such relationships being baptised.

First, it is argued, those who are in same-sex sexual relationships need to be baptised (just like anyone else) and that they can be baptised in the sense that they can receive baptism with water in the name of the Trinity and make the baptismal promises.

Secondly, because only God can see the secrets of people's hearts, we are not in a position to say that someone who is in a same-sex sexual relationship (or anyone else) is not sincere in their desire to be baptised, or in their willingness to make the baptismal promises. Having made sure that people have been instructed about the meaning of baptism and the seriousness of the promises they will make, we have to take people at their word – just as we do, for example, when people make their wedding vows.

Thirdly, we cannot say that because someone has not yet turned away from sin in one area of their life then any profession of repentance that they make is therefore insincere. All of us that we have areas of our life in which we do not yet live as we should (see 1 John 1:8–10). However, this does not mean that our repentance and faith are not real. None of us are without sin now and none of us will ever be without sin this side of eternity. If repentance involving total freedom from sin was a prerequisite for baptism, then no one would ever reach the stage where they could be baptised. It is therefore unjust to single out a special category of sexual sinner and say they cannot be baptised while other sinners can be.

Fourthly, looking at the same point from a different angle, it is sometimes suggested that if adults who are in a same-sex sexual relationship are baptised, this means that the church is in some way endorsing their sexual behaviour. This is not the case. Baptism is not a merit mark for godly behaviour. The reason people are baptised is not because they are good and therefore deserving of a reward, but because they not good and need God's grace given in baptism in order to become good.

If the members of a church think baptising someone in a same-sex sexual relationship is an endorsement of their behaviour, then this is a reason for giving them further instruction about the meaning of baptism. It is not a reason for not baptising the person concerned.

Fifthly, as John Bunyan makes clear in *The Pilgrim's Progress,* the Christian life is a journey from this life to the next in which we are meant to grow in holiness of life through the grace of God and the prayers, guidance and support of our Christian brothers and sisters. If we feel (as we should) that someone in a same-sex sexual relationship, or anyone else, needs to grow in holiness of life then we need to get them started on the Christian journey and this means encouraging them to be baptised rather than refusing them baptism.

Moving on to the issue of the baptism of children, those who take this second approach would say that there are also a number of reasons why it is right to baptise children for whom those in same-sex sexual relationships have parental responsibility.

First, these children need the gift God offers in baptism just as much as any other child. They too need to die with Christ and rise to new life in him. This means we have an obligation to baptise them if this is at all possible.[18]

Secondly, there is no reason why it is impossible to baptise such children:

- They can receive baptism with water in the name of the Trinity

- The baptismal promises can be made on their behalf by their sureties

- They can ratify and confirm those promises when they reach the years of discretion and live a baptised life of repentance and faith

Thirdly, it is not the cases that baptising a child involves affirming the status of the relationship between the adults who are responsible for them. Infant baptism is about the relationship between a particular child and God, not the about relationship between the adults who are responsible for them.

Fourthly, just as the moral unworthiness of the minister who performed a baptism would not hinder its spiritual efficacy, so also the moral unworthiness of those speaking for a child at their baptism would not hinder its spiritual efficacy either.[19] What matters for the efficacy of baptism is that the promises are objectively made and that the child concerned ratifies and confirms them when they are old enough to do so.

Fifthly, the idea that a child would be implicated in any sin committed by those adults who took part in their baptism goes

---

[18] It is because it is important to baptise children if at all possible that the rubric for infant baptism in the *Book of Common Prayer* and Canon B22 both prohibit a minister from refusing to baptise an infant within their cure. This would include refusing to baptise a child because of their family circumstances.

[19] See Article XXVI of the *Thirty-Nine Articles*, 1571.

against the clear biblical teaching that people are responsible for their own sins and not for the sins of others. 'The soul that sins shall die. The son shall not suffer for the iniquity of the father, nor the father suffer for the iniquity of the son; the righteousness of the righteous shall be upon himself, and the wickedness of the wicked shall be upon himself' (Ezekiel 18:20,).

Finally, we cannot know for certain how any couple with parental responsibilities (whether in a same-sex relationship or otherwise) will bring up a child. However, what we do know is that, if baptism is refused, a child will definitely not be brought up to ratify and confirm the baptismal promises for themselves since they will never have been made.

It should be noted that taking Approach B, like those taking Approach A, would use the time of instruction allowed under Canon B22.4 to explain to those seeking baptism why same-sex sexual relationships are incompatible with faithful Christian discipleship.

It should also be noted that Approach B would not involve accepting godparents who were in same-sex sexual relationships. Canon B23.2 states: 'The godparents shall be persons who will faithfully fulfil their responsibilities by their care for the children committed to their charge and by the example of their own godly living.'[20]

Those in same-sex sexual relationships cannot not provide an example of 'godly living' and for this reason must be regarded as disqualified from being godparents.

---

[20] Canon B.23.2, *The Canons of the Church of England* 7th edition (London: Church House Publishing, 2016.

The issue of what goes in the baptism register

For those who take Approach A, the issue of who should be listed as parents in the baptism register simply does not arise.

For those who take Approach B, the question of what should go in baptism registers when two people of the same sex have parental responsibility is a legal rather than a theological issue. However much they may feel that children should have two parents of the opposite sex, the fact is that there are same-sex couples who have shared parental responsibility for children and who are therefore legally their mothers or fathers. What goes in the baptism register merely reflects this legal reality. It does not endorse the family situation involved.

Conclusion

The current position of the Church of England is to baptise both adults in same-sex sexual relationships and children for whom parents in same-sex sexual relationships have parental responsibility.

As we have seen, the argument put forward by the House of Bishops that the sincerity of the convictions of lay people in same-sex relationships justifies the current practice is unconvincing. We have to start from the basis that, whatever those in same-sex sexual relationships believe, such relationships are objectively sinful.

As we have also seen, those who start from this basis take two different approaches to the question of whether those in same-sex sexual relationships, or the children for whom they are responsible, can rightly be baptised.

What those in the Church of England need to do is think carefully about which of these positions is the correct one so that an agreed position can be developed which reflects biblical truth. Both approaches involve potentially serious spiritual consequences if they are wrong, and so we cannot say it does not matter which one the Church of England follows. The truth about the issue matters and so we need to reach agreement about what the truth is.

It should be noted, however, that even if Approach B is the correct approach, the reasons for holding it have absolutely nothing to do with theological acceptance of same-sex sexual relationships or support for same-sex marriage.

This means that contrary to what is said by Bishop David, there is nothing 'ironic' about the fact that baptism 'is open to all whereas lawfully married same sex couples are barred from both a church marriage and the possibility of ordination.'[21] The Church of England would being perfectly consistent if it continued to say in accordance with Approach B that it will baptise people who are in same-sex sexual relationships and those children for whom they have a parental responsibility, but that it will not ordain or marry them.

---

[21] Gillett, 'Does the Bible Really Say...that Baptism Should be Withheld from Some People?'.

10. Why Creation is 'Straight'

In the final essay of the 'Does the Bible Really Say...?' series, Dr Simon Taylor looks at the question, 'Does the Bible Really Say...that Creation is Straight?'[1]

Dr Taylor's argument

In the introductory paragraphs to his essay, Dr Taylor explains that the idea that 'creation is straight' is his shorthand for the 'complementarian' understanding of creation 'in which human beings are made and meant to be male and female.'[2]

Dr Taylor then further explains that he is 'far from convinced that this is the right way to be reading Scripture' and that in his essay he is going to 'look at some key Biblical texts and then to see if a larger Biblical vision might be offered.'[3]

The three biblical texts he looks at are Genesis 1:27–28, Genesis 2:18–24 and Matthew 19:3–9.

Genesis 1:27–28

On Genesis 1:27–28 Dr Taylor notes that:

> A complementarian reading of this passage attends carefully to the way in which the image of God structures humanity as male and female. Combined

---

[1] Simon Taylor, 'Does the Bible Does the Bible Really Say...that Creation is Straight?', 18 July 2019,
at https://viamedia.news/2019/07/18/does-the-bible-really-say-that-creation-is-straight/ (accessed 14 April 2020).
[2] Taylor, 'Does the Bible Does the Bible Really Say...that Creation is Straight?'.
[3] Taylor, 'Does the Bible Does the Bible Really Say...that Creation is Straight?'.

with the injunction to procreation, this is then taken to require heterosexual relationships.[1]

He then identifies three 'serious difficulties with this approach':

> First, it is in danger of requiring couplings of male and female in order to display the image of God. What then do we have to say for single people?

> Second, it takes the command to 'be fruitful and multiply' as a command for every couple, rather than for the species as a whole. What then of the childless, the elderly and the infertile?

> Third, it loses the way the passage insists that the image of God is seen in women as well as in men. This has not, through the history of humanity and the history of the Church, been something seen as obvious. Sexual relationships have been constituted as expressions of male power, underwritten by a male God. Genesis 1.27–28 begs to differ.[2]

Genesis 2:18–24

On Genesis 2:18–24, Dr Taylor comments that this text:

> has also been taken to support a complementarian account of human relationships. The 'one flesh' that derives from marriage is taken to require a man and a woman.[3]

---

[1] Taylor, 'Does the Bible Does the Bible Really Say...that Creation is Straight?'.

[2] Taylor, 'Does the Bible Does the Bible Really Say...that Creation is Straight?'.

[3] Taylor, 'Does the Bible Does the Bible Really Say...that Creation is Straight?'.

As before, he identifies three problems with this complementarian reading:

> First, the 'one flesh' that Genesis 2.24 speaks about is an expression of kinship, not of sexual relations. 'One flesh' could be polygamous, and often is in the Old Testament. Despite this being the 'go-to text' for monogamy, the marriage envisioned is not simply the pairing of a man and a woman.
>
> Second, the order in which the man and woman are created has been taken to imply the subordination of women, 1 Timothy 2.11–15 being a prime example. Yet we have already seen that Genesis 1.27–28 is seeking to deny such subordination.
>
> Third, Genesis 2.24 needs to be read as part of the whole story, which begins at verse 18. To read the final verse in isolation misses the whole point of the story.
>
> In the story of Genesis 2, God creates the animals so that the 'man' (adam), the first human person, should not be alone. As the first human names the animals, none is found to be a helper and partner. But there is a real sense that they might have been. Then God creates woman from the flesh of the first human. Again, the human names the creature woman ('ishah) and names himself man ('ish).
>
> The force of the story is on the consent of the person, and the delight of the man in the woman. Consent and delight are what structures this story. Gareth Moore writes of 'the final bankruptcy of the compulsory heterosexuality interpretation of the story of Adam and Eve. Not only does it misrepresent God as one who imposes his will regardless of human delight, but

... it completely undermines the dynamic that leads to the creation of Eve.'[4]

Matthew 19:3–9

On Matthew 19:3–9 Dr Taylor explains that those who take a complementarian position hold that these verses give:

> the authority of Jesus to their interpretations of Genesis, and does so clearly in a discussion about marriage. When Jesus speaks of marriage, they argue, he does so in a complementarian model of male and female.[5]

However, as he sees it:

> nothing in this passage that changes the force of the readings I have offered of the two Genesis passages. Indeed, I would be happy to see Jesus reinforcing the assertion of Genesis 1 that women are fully human, and the assertions of Genesis 2 that consent and joy are at the heart of all human relationships. Nothing that Jesus says in Matthew's account need be understood as requiring a complementarian account of human beings.[6]

---

[4] The reference is to Gareth Moore OP, *A Question of Truth: Christianity and Homosexuality* (London and New York: Continuum, 2003), p. 143.

[5] Taylor, 'Does the Bible Does the Bible Really Say...that Creation is Straight?'.

[6] Taylor, 'Does the Bible Does the Bible Really Say...that Creation is Straight?'.

A larger biblical vision

In the final section of his paper, in which he sets out a 'larger biblical vision', he criticises N T Wright's view that the Bible is:

> an entire narrative which works with this complementarity so that a male-plus-female marriage is a signpost or a signal about the goodness of the original creation and God's intention for the eventual new heavens and new earth.[7]

Dr Taylor comments that his readings of these three biblical passages explain why he thinks Wright is wrong to read the Bible as saying that humans are created to be 'male-plus-female'. Taylor then notes that passages such as Isaiah 62:4–5 and Revelation 19:6–9, which link marriage and the new creation, describe God's people as 'female, as a bride.'[8]

This last point is significant, argues Dr Taylor, because:

> If we read from the Scriptures to the people of God without any further thought or insight, we might find ourselves requiring all God's people to be female. Rather than arguing about whether women can take leadership roles in the Church, or whether we can have women bishops, we might find we need books and articles explaining why men can be Christians at all. The image of the bride is gendered.
>
> Yet I am not aware of any theologian or interpreter of the Bible that has taken that image as determining the

---

[7] Taylor, 'Does the Bible Does the Bible Really Say...that Creation is Straight?', quoting from Matthew Schmitz, 'N. T. Wright on Gay Marriage: Nature and narrative point to complementarity', 11 June 2014, https://www.firstthings.com/blogs/firstthoughts/2014/06/n-t-wrights-%20argument-against-same-sex-marriage (accessed 14 April 2020).

[8] Taylor, 'Does the Bible Does the Bible Really Say...that Creation is Straight?'.

gender of individuals within the people of God. Even if the creation narratives do speak of a complementary relationship between male and female at the heart of creation, it is a quite different theological move to require such a relationship of every individual person or couple within God's people.[9]

To put it simply, just as Isaiah and Revelation don't require all God's people to be female, so also the creation narratives do not require everyone to be in a relationship with someone of the opposite sex.

A better approach to reading the Bible, Dr Taylor suggests, is to start from Ephesians 2:13–22. This passage tells us that:

> At the heart of God's purposes is the bringing together of all things and all people, however far off they may once have seemed. The death of Christ brings everyone into one new humanity, putting hostility to death. All are reconciled to God in one body, and no one is a stranger or an alien, but citizens and saints.[10]

The picture given in this passage, he writes,

> is one of the fullness of God and of creation, with all things reconciled and built together into a place where God can live. There is difference, but it is reconciled, no longer requiring hostility between different groups. And there is a wide range of difference that has been reconciled: male and female, Jew and gentile, married and single, different races and

---

9 Taylor, 'Does the Bible Does the Bible Really Say...that Creation is Straight?'.
10 Taylor, 'Does the Bible Does the Bible Really Say...that Creation is Straight?'.

nations, people of different sexualities and different gender identities.[11]

Dr Taylor's final conclusion is that:

> The Bible calls us to a bigger and fuller vision of God and his creation. But that vision is not structured by human relationships, but by Christ in whom 'the whole structure is joined together and grows into a holy temple in the Lord; in whom you also are built together spiritually into a dwelling-place for God' (Ephesians 2.21–22).
>
> Complementarian readings of Scripture are in danger of getting this the wrong way round, which results in structuring Christ around human relationships. To limit the Biblical vision to a simple 'male-plus-female' is to limit the creative and reconciling power of God.
>
> Creation is not straight, it is full of difference, all of which is reconciled into one new humanity through Jesus.[12]

What are we to make of Dr Taylor's argument?

Genesis 1:27–28

Looking at Genesis 1:27–28 first of all, the text clearly does say that God structured humanity as male and female: 'So God created man in his own image, in the image of God he created him; male and female he created them' (Genesis 1:27, – and the same point is repeated in Genesis 5:1–2). It also clearly links the way that God has structured humanity as male and female to the command to 'Be fruitful and multiply' (Genesis 1:28,).

---

[11] Taylor, 'Does the Bible Does the Bible Really Say...that Creation is Straight?'.

[12] Taylor, 'Does the Bible Does the Bible Really Say...that Creation is Straight?'.

It is because human beings are male and female that they can be commanded to be fruitful and multiply. Sex (as in the difference between male and female) and sex (as in the act of sexual intercourse leading to the procreation of children) go together.

However, this does not mean that single people are not made in the image of God. Someone is made in the image of God as a male or female human being, not as part of married couple. Genesis 1 does not suggest that people becomes God's image bearers only when they get married.

The command to be fruitful and multiply is a command to human beings in general, and obeying this command is an integral part of what marriage is about. As the Christian tradition has always insisted, the procreation of children is a central part of what marriage is for. To use the traditional language, it is one of the 'goods' of marriage. We can see this in Genesis 2–5 where Adam and Eve are brought together by God in the first marriage and it is in this God-given context that they then obey the command to be fruitful and multiply (Genesis 4:1, 2, 25, 5:3).

However, this does not mean that childless couples, or those incapable of having children, are not truly married. The key questions about childless marriages are (a) whether their form of relationship is one that would have led to children being born in the absence of accidental factors such as age, or a medical problem resulting in an inability to conceive, and (b) whether the couple would welcome any children granted to them by God as a result of their union? If the answer to both questions was 'yes', then a childless marriage would fall within the scope God's intentions for marriage. The couple would be seeking to live as God has ordained. That is why in the Bible, the childless marriages of Abram and Sarai (Genesis 12:2, 18:11) and Zechariah and Elizabeth (Luke 1:7) are still described as marriages.

Dr Taylor's last point – that a complementarian reading of Genesis 1 loses sight of the fact that the text says that women are made in the image of God just as much as men – is completely baffling. Why would the claim that Genesis 1 says that God created human beings as male and female and that fulfilling the command to be fruitful and multiply requires relationships between men and woman imply that women are not made in God's image? This simply does not follow.

It may indeed be the case that, historically, sexual relationships have been viewed in terms of the exercise of male power, as Dr Taylor says, but there is nothing in a complementarian reading of Genesis 1 that leads to this view.

Genesis 2:18–24

The first point to make in regard to Dr Taylor's reading of this text is that he is mistaken when he argues that 'one flesh' implies kinship rather than a sexual relationship. Flesh is used in Scripture to mean kinship, but in Genesis 2 the reference to 'one flesh' in 2:24 references back to the statement by Adam in the previous verse following the creation of Eve: 'this at last is bone of my bones and flesh of my flesh' (Genesis 2:23,). The one flesh union between a man a woman in marriage is seen In Genesis as the coming together of the two separate halves of the human race (the two elements of human flesh) in a sexual union that will enable procreation and thus the fulfilment of the command to 'be fruitful and multiply'.

Furthermore, the relationship envisaged in Genesis 2:24 is monogamous rather than polygamous. The paradigmatic relationship ordained by God between Adam and Eve is a monogamous one and in similar fashion in Genesis 2:24 a man 'cleaves to his wife' not 'wives'. Polygamy does not come into the picture until we get the story of Lamech in Genesis 4:17–24 in which Lamech having multiple wives is a demonstration of the spreading effects of sin after the Fall.

Secondly, there is not, as Dr Taylor seems to suggest, a link between a belief that 'one flesh' refers to a sexual union between a man and a woman and a belief that women are (or should be) subordinate to men. The two beliefs are entirely distinct, which is why numerous Christians who take an egalitarian view of the relationship between women and men continue to understand 'one flesh' in a traditional way.

It should also be noted that holding that there is a God-given order in the relationship between men and women does not mean holding that women are not equal in their humanity to men. Thus Geoffrey Bromiley comments on Genesis 2:

> The male has a certain priority in this relation, for the woman is taken from the man and not the other way round. Yet priority is not the point of the story. The equal humanity which is needed for full companionship takes precedence. As in the Trinity, the Father, as the fount of deity, has a certain precedence over the Son and the Spirit, yet all are equally God in eternal interrelation, so it is with man and woman in the fellowship which God has purposed and created.[13]

Thirdly, it is simply not the case, as Dr Taylor argues following Gareth Moore, that the text implies that the animals 'might have been' a suitable partner for Adam and that what makes the difference with Eve is simply that Adam delights in her rather than them.

Dr Taylor is correct to say that Genesis 2:24 needs to be read in the light of the whole section consisting of verses 18–24. However, what he fails to acknowledge is that Genesis 2 needs to be read in the light of Genesis 1:26–28. In terms of the literary structure of Genesis, Genesis 2 is narrative commentary on what is said in Genesis 1 about God creating

---

[13] Geoffrey Bromiley, *God and Marriage* (Grand Rapids: Eerdmans, 1980), p. 3.

humanity as male and female. Genesis 2 is a story that explains why human beings need to both male and female.

The key statement in the story is God's statement in verse 18, 'I will make a helper fit for him.' As Ian Paul notes, the Hebrew word *kenegdo* translated 'fit for him' in the RSV:

> has the sense of equal but opposite; it is the kind of phrase you might use to describe the opposite bank of a river, combining both the sense of equality and difference and distinctiveness.[14]

In Genesis 2:20, we are told none of the non-human creatures surveyed by Adam were a suitable helper because they were 'not...fit for him. (Genesis 2:20). They did not meet the criteria of being equal yet distinct. The reason Eve does then fit the bill (and the reason Adam delights in her) is that she is equal as another human being ('bone of my bones and flesh of my flesh', Genesis 2:23) but different in that she is a woman rather than another man.

The story is indeed about 'consent and delight' but it is consent and delight to God's good ordering of humanity as male and female.

Matthew 19:3–9

Dr Taylor once more misses the point of biblical text in his account of Matthew 19:3–9. The text is not about Jesus affirming that 'women are fully human' or that 'consent and joy are at the heart of all human relationships.'[15] What the text is about is Jesus affirming that God created human beings as male and female, that he created marriage as a relationship between a man and a woman, and that because a married couple are joined together by God human beings should not break their marriage apart.

---

[14] Paul, *Same-sex Unions*, p. 8.
[15] Taylor, 'Does the Bible Does the Bible Really Say...that Creation is Straight?'.

Contrary to what Dr Taylor asserts, what Jesus gives us in Matthew 19 is indeed a 'complementarian account of human beings' since it affirms that 'human beings are made and meant to be male and female.'[16]

A larger biblical vision

Dr Taylor's response to N T Wright is unsatisfactory in two ways.

First, as we have seen, nothing that Dr Taylor has said has called into question the correctness of Wright's claim that the biblical narrative works on the basis of a God-given complementarity of 'male-plus-female'.

As the American writer Michael Brown notes, 'the Bible is a heterosexual book':[17]

- every single reference to marriage in the entire Bible speaks of heterosexual unions, without exception, to the point that a Hebrew idiom for marriage is for a man to 'take a wife'

- every warning to men about sexual purity presupposes heterosexuality, with a married man often warned not to lust after another woman

- every discussion about family order and structure speaks explicitly in heterosexual terms, referring to husbands and wives, fathers and mothers

- every law or instruction given to children presupposes heterosexuality, as children are urged to heed, or obey, or follow, the counsel or example of their father and mother

- every parable, illustration, or metaphor having to do with marriage is presented in exclusively heterosexual terms

---

[16] Taylor, 'Does the Bible Does the Bible Really Say...that Creation is Straight?'.
[17] Brown, *Can you be Gay and Christian?*.

- in the Old Testament, God depicts his relationship with Israel as that of a groom and a bride; and in the New Testament, the image shifts to the marital union of husband and wife as a picture of Christ and the church

- since there was no such thing as *in vitro* fertilisation and the like in biblical times, the only parents were heterosexual (it still takes a man and woman to produce a child), and there is not a hint of homosexual couples adopting children[18]

Secondly, Dr Taylor is wrong to conflate the two issues of (a) the metaphorical use of the term 'bride' or 'wife' to refer to the relationship between God and his people, and (b) whether the complementarity between male and female has to extend to every human relationship.

Because the use of the terms 'bride' and 'wife' are metaphorical, it does not follow that every member of the church has to be female (any more than the use of the metaphor 'shepherd' for God means that all members of the church are sheep). However, the way that God has created the world, to which the Bible bears witness, does mean that every human being needs to be in some form of relationship with members of the opposite sex, and that marriage (and hence sexual relations) should be between a man and a woman.

The problem with Dr Taylor's proposal to ground a vision of 'God and his creation' in the account of reconciliation in Ephesians 2:13–22 is that this passage does not exist in isolation. It forms part of the bigger biblical canon and has to be read in the light of this fact.

When we read the passage in this context, we discover that the God to whom Ephesians refers – the Triune God who has reconciled us to himself in Christ – is the same God who created human beings as male and female and who ordained that marriage should be between a man and a woman.

---

[18] Brown, *Can you be Gay and Christian?*, pp. 88–89.

Furthermore, the humans whom God reconciles are the human beings whom God has created in this way and for whom marriage has been ordained in this way.

It is therefore a poor reading of Scripture to contrast reconciliation and complementarity as contrasting approaches to understanding what the Bible says. They are two facets of the biblical picture and both need to be accepted. We are both those who have been created as male and female and are called to live rightly in the light of this fact, and those who have been reconciled to God in Christ.

It should also be noted that the Bible does not talk about the reconciliation of 'people of different sexualities and different gender identities.'[19] The Bible does not see 'sexualities' in ontological terms as much modern thinking does. From a biblical perspective people are not lesbian, gay, bi, trans, questioning, etc. They are simply men or women and called to live as such. Furthermore, the Bible does not think in terms of 'gender identities' either. To repeat, in the Bible there are simply men and women.

Conclusion

It is indeed true, as Dr Taylor says, that 'creation is full of difference.'[20] Humans are different from the non-human creation (which is itself hugely diverse) and all humans are different from each other. Nevertheless, 'creation is straight' in the sense that the world in which this difference exists is one in which 'human beings are made and meant to be male and female.'[21]

---

[19] Taylor, 'Does the Bible Does the Bible Really Say...that Creation is Straight?'.
[20] Taylor, 'Does the Bible Does the Bible Really Say...that Creation is Straight?'.
[21] Taylor, 'Does the Bible Does the Bible Really Say...that Creation is Straight?'.

Appended note – those who are intersex

An obvious objection to what I have said in this chapter is the existence of intersex people who, it is claimed, fall outside of the binary divide between male and female.

The first point to note in this regard is that the number of people who are genuinely intersex in the sense that their bodies are a mixture of male and female biology either at the level of their genotype (their genetic constitution) or their phenotype (their observable physical characteristics) is a tiny proportion of the population as a whole – some 0.018% of live births.[22] To put it the other way around, this means that more than 99.98% of human beings are clearly either male or female. By any reasonable definition of what counts as 'normal', being either male or female is overwhelmingly normal for human beings. It follows that any argument against the traditional Christian division of humanity into male and female that depends on the claim that intersex conditions are relatively common is untenable. True intersex conditions are very rare indeed.

It should also be noted that those with the medical conditions involved are not neither male not female, they are a combination of male *and* female. Furthermore this combination is, medically speaking, a disorder of development, what Oliver O'Donovan has called 'an ambiguity which has arisen by a malfunction in a dimorphic human sexual pattern.'[23]

However, acknowledgement that such conditions exist still leaves us with the task of thinking about the specific

---

[22] Leonard Sax, How common is intersex?', *Journal of Sex Research*, 1 August 2002, http://www.leonardsax.com/how-common-is-intersex-a-response-to-anne-fausto-sterling/ (accessed 18 April 2020).
[23] Oliver O'Donovan, *Transsexualism: Issues and argument* (Cambridge: Grove Books, 2007), p. 8.

possibilities of vocation for people who are affected by them. How can they live rightly before God as the people they are?

Firstly, it must be emphasised once again that, like all other human beings, people with intersex conditions first and foremost human beings made in God's image and likeness. The statement 'Christians United in Support of LGBT+ Inclusion in the Church' is right to declare, 'We affirm that those who are born as intersex are full and equal bearers of the image and likeness of God and are worthy of full dignity and respect.'[24] Even though the development of their male or female identity has become disordered, people with intersex conditions bear witness to their creation as human beings in God's image and likeness through the male and female elements that exist in their genotype and phenotype.

Secondly, they, like all other human beings, are summoned to live as people created by God and redeemed by God through Jesus Christ, having faith in the gospel, loving God and neighbour, and living lives marked by the offering and receiving of friendship.

Thirdly, they, like all other human beings, are summoned to live in a way that reflects God's creation of humanity as male and female. In cases where there is distinct male or female genotype but where problems have occurred in the development of the corresponding phenotype, the proper way forward would seem to be for them to live according to the sex of their genotype, receiving spiritual and psychological support and (where necessary) medical intervention in the form of reconstructive surgery to help them live more comfortably in their given sex and, when possible, to allow them to have children. Just like everyone else they may either be called to

---

[24] 'Christians United in Support of LGBT+ Inclusion in the Church,' Article 4, at
https://www.patheos.com/blogs/mercynotsacrifice/2017/08/30/chr istians-united-statement-support-lgbt-inclusion/ accessed 21 November 2020.

marry a member of the opposite sex, or be called to serve God through a life of singleness.

In the very rare cases where the genotype has both XY and XX chromosomes and the phenotype has both male and female sexual characteristics (for example both a penis and a vagina), the question of whether it would be proper to live as male or female becomes much less clear cut.

A possible way forward that would bear witness to the truth of who they are would be for them to choose to live as either male or female. They would thus respond to God's general call to humans to live as a man or a woman while acknowledging the presence of elements of the other sex in their bodily make up. If this way forward were adopted, then any marriage would need to be with a member of the opposite sex to that in which they have chosen to live. What would arguably not be appropriate would be for them to live as a non-binary person (in other words, neither male nor female). This is because the truth about who they are is not that they are neither male nor female, but that the way their biology has developed means that they are both male and female.

11. CONCLUSION

This collection of essays is limited in scope. It does not address the full range of issues that exist in relation to sexuality, marriage and family life. It also says very little about the vital issue of the pastoral care that should be offered to those who are same-sex attracted, or who are in same-sex relationships. [1]

What it does do is show that a number of the arguments that are commonly brought against the traditional Christian sexual ethic are unconvincing.

In his book *Mere Christianity* C S Lewis writes 'the Christian rule is: 'Either marriage, with complete faithfulness to your partner, or else total abstinence." By the term 'marriage' Lewis means a marriage between one man and one woman, and what we have seen is that nothing contained in the essays from ViaMedia.News shows that Christians today have any good reason to dissent from the Christian rule as Lewis describes it.

Therefore, when Christians hear people saying 'Does the Bible really say?' in relation to the Church's traditional teaching with regard to sex and marriage, the robust answer they should give is 'Yes it does.'

Yes. it does say, just as nature does, that God created the human race as male and female.

Yes, it does say that God has ordained marriage between one man and one woman as the proper context for sexual intercourse and the begetting and raising of children.

Yes, it does say that all forms of sexual intercourse outside marriage are contrary to God's will.

We cannot evade the fact that the Bible says these things. We need to accept them, live by them ourselves, teach them to others, and stand lovingly and prayerfully alongside those who,

---

[1] For a helpful introduction to this issue see Ed Shaw *The Plausibility Problem: The Church and Same-Sex Attraction* (London: IVP, 2015).

for whatever reason, find them particularly difficult, assuring them that God loves then, and that he is always there for them, constantly offering them forgiveness and a fresh start with him.

'The steadfast love of the Lord never ceases,
his mercies never come to an end;
they are new every morning.'
 (Lamentations 3:22-23)

BIBLIOGRAPHY

Sam Allberry, *Is God Anti-gay?* (Epsom: The Good Book Company, 2013).

Michael Brown, *Can you be Gay and Christian?* (Lake Mary: Front Line, 2014).

Richard Davidson, *Flame of Yahweh – Sexuality in the Old Testament* (Peabody: Hendrickson, 2007).

Martin Davie, *Glorify God in your Body* (London: CEEC, 2018).

Martin Davie, *Studies on the Bible and Same-sex Relationships Since 2003* (Malton: Gilead Books, 2015).

Sean Doherty, *The Only Way is Ethics – Part 1: Sex and Marriage* (Milton Keynes: Authentic, 2015).

S. Donald Fortson III and Rollin G. Grams, *Unchanging Witness: The Consistent Christian Teaching on Homosexuality and Tradition* (Nashville: B&H Academic, 2016).

Robert Gagnon, *The Bible and Homosexual Practice* (Nashville: Abingdon Press 2001).

Richard Hays, *The Moral Vision of the New Testament* (Edinburgh: T&T Clark, 1996).

William Loader, *The New Testament on Sexuality* (Grands Rapids and Cambridge: Eerdmans 2012).

Ian Paul, *Same-sex Unions: The Key Biblical Texts* (Cambridge: Grove Books, 2014).

John Stott, *Same Sex Relationships* (Epsom: Good Book Company, 2017).

Donald Wold, *Out of Order* (Grand Rapids: Baker, 1998).

Useful material can also be found on the following websites:

Living Out (https://www.livingout.org/)

True Freedom Trust (https://truefreedomtrust.co.uk/)

The Anglican Foundations Series

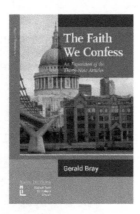

The Anglican Foundations series is a collection of books which offer practical guidance on Church of England services in the Book of Common Prayer.

These include:

- The Faith We Confess – An exposition of the Thirty-Nine Articles
- The 'Very Pure Word of God – The Book of Common Prayer as a model of biblical liturgy
- Dearly Beloved – Building God's people through morning and evening prayer
- Day by Day – The rhythm of the Bible in the Book of Common Prayer
- The Supper – Cranmer and Communion
- A Fruitful Exhortation – A guide to the Homilies
- Instruction in the Way of the Lord – A guide to the catechism
- Till Death Do Us Part – "The solemnization of Matrimony" in the Book of Common Prayer
- Sure and Certain Hope – Death and burial
- The Athanasian Creed
- The Anglican Ordinal
- "Doubt Not...But Earnestly Believe" – A Fresh Look at the BCP Bapstism Service

'Doubt not...But Earnestly Believe' A Fresh Look at the BCP Baptist Service by *Mark Pickles*

Whilst Common Worship (2000) provides a Book of Common Prayer Communion (BCP) in modern English, sadly there is no such provision for the BCP baptism service. For some Anglican evangelicals this may not seem to be a particularly regrettable omission.

There are those who might not be persuaded of the biblical mandate for baptising infants, whilst others might have concerns over some of the language used that may appear to affirm 'baptismal regeneration'. This booklet is an attempt not only to engage with those questions and concerns but also to proffer an enthusiastic support for the theology and liturgical content of the BCP Baptism service. It has a great emphasis on the covenantal grace of God which encourages Christian parents to "doubt not – but earnestly believe" in God's faithfulness and mercy. In so doing it directs our primary focus to our promise keeping God and not to ourselves.

The Anglican Ordinal: Gospel Priorities for Church of England Ministry by *Andrew Atherstone*

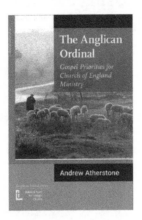

This book is part of our *Anglican Foundations* series, which offers practical guidance on Church of England services.

There is no better handbook for Anglican ministry than the Anglican ordinal – the authorized liturgy for ordaining new ministers. The ordinal contains a beautiful, succinct description of theological priorities and ministry models for today's Church. This booklet offers a simple exposition of the ordinal's primary themes. Anglican clergy are called to public ministry as messengers, sentinels, stewards, and shepherds. They are asked searching questions and they make solemn promises. The Holy Spirit's anointing is invoked upon their ministries, with the laying-on-of-hands, and they are given a Bible as the visual symbol of their new pastoral and preaching office. This booklet is a handy primer for ordinands and clergy, and all those responsible for their selection, training, and deployment.

Thomas Cranmer: Using the Bible to Evangelize the Nation by *Peter Adam*

We need not only to do evangelism, but also to develop contemporary gospel strategies which we trust, under God, will be effective. We need gospel wisdom, as well as gospel work. We need to work on local evangelism, but also work on God's global gospel plan. This alerts us to our own nation, as well as other nations. Gospel strategy includes the question, 'How should we evangelise our nation?' Thomas Cranmer, Archbishop of Canterbury 1532-56, strategised and worked to do this from the perspective of Anglican Reformed theology and practice. We cannot duplicate his plan in detail, but he can inspire us, and also teach us the key ingredients of such a plan.

His context of ministry had advantages and disadvantages! Our context has the same mixture. We can also learn from Cranmer's ability to work effectively in his context, despite the many problems, and the suffering he endured. God used him to evangelise his nation at his time. May God use us for his gospel glory!

Focus on Jesus: A Guide to the Message of Handel's Messiah by *Robert Bashford*

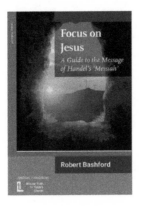

This book provides a commentary on the message of *Messiah*. Handel's great oratorio gives a marvellous portrayal of the Person and Work of Jesus Christ: the anticipation of his coming, his birth, his ministry, his sufferings and death, his resurrection and his ascension – plus also the proclamation of the Gospel to the world, and Christian assurance of resurrection life beyond death.

The main focus of this study is the selection of Bible verses that make up the work, compiled by the librettist Charles Jennens. At the same time there is also a certain amount of comment on the music, showing how Handel's distinctive skill contributes towards clearly expressing the message.

The aim of the book is that readers may deepen their understanding of the Bible passages included in the work, and enjoy Handel's *Messiah* all the more – and as a result know Christ better.

Lightning Source UK Ltd.
Milton Keynes UK
UKHW011828010223
416326UK00001B/7